FEAR STRIKES OUT

The Jim Piersall Story

BY

Jim Piersall and Al Hirshberg

WITH A NEW AFTERWORD BY

Jim Piersall

UNIVERSITY OF NEBRASKA PRESS
LINCOLN AND LONDON

⊗

First Bison Books printing: 1999
Most recent printing indicated by the last digit below:
10   9   8   7   6   5   4   3   2   1

Library of Congress Cataloging-in-Publication Data
Piersall, Jimmy.
Fear strikes out: the Jim Piersall story / by Jim Piersall and Al
Hirshberg; with a new afterword by Jim Piersall.
p.   cm.
Originally published: Boston: Little, Brown, 1955.
ISBN 0-8032-8761-5 (pbk.: alk. paper)
1. Piersall, Jimmy.   2. Baseball players—United States—
Biography.   I. Hirshberg, Albert, 1909–1973.   II. Title.
III. Title: Jim Piersall story.
GV865.P54A34   1999
797.357′092—dc21
[B]
98-49645   CIP

Fear Strikes Out

Fear Strikes Out

I MUST have been quite a card when first I broke into baseball's big league as a Boston Red Sox rookie in 1952. That spring, besides playing good ball, I convulsed the fans with my antics. I was a funny man, a baseball clown, and wherever the Red Sox went, the fans flocked to see me. My repertoire of pantomime and slapstick made me a ripe subject for sports writers and columnists.

Almost everybody except the umpires and the Red Sox thought I was a riot. My wife knew I was sick, yet she was helpless to stop my mad rush towards a mental collapse. The Red Sox couldn't figure out how to handle me. I was a problem child. The umpires, whom I plagued with silly protests over routine decisions, thought I was a pain in the neck.

Lou Boudreau, the Red Sox manager, never knew whether to play me or to keep me on the bench. He liked the way I played ball but not the way I behaved. When he played me I clowned so outrageously that I threatened to make a travesty of the game. When he didn't, I badgered him to distraction. Sometimes I stormed and screamed if I couldn't play, and once I even cried in public like a baby. I mocked my teammates and fought with them and with opposing players. I had the whole club, and indeed, much of the American League, in an uproar. Finally the Red Sox sent me to their Southern Association farm club at Birmingham, Alabama, but I was worse there than I had been in Boston. Then I returned to Boston, where the roof suddenly fell in on me. I went berserk one day, and ended up in a mental institution.

I don't remember any of it. From the moment I walked into the lobby of the Sarasota-Terrace Hotel in Sarasota, Florida, to report to the Red Sox special training camp on the morning of January 15, 1952, until the moment I came to my senses in the violent room of the Westborough State Hospital in Massachusetts the following August, my mind is almost an absolute blank. I do have a clear recollection of the birth of my second daughter, Doreen, in March, but outside of that, there are only a few hazy impressions.

But I pulled out of it. Shock treatments, faith, a wonderful wife, a fine doctor and loyal friends pulled me out of it. I pulled out of it so well that I was sound and healthy by the spring of 1953. I pulled out of it so well that I was named the outstanding sophomore ballplayer in the American League. I now face the future with confidence, for I know that I have recovered completely, just as surely as if I had recovered completely from pneumonia or chickenpox or a broken leg instead of mental illness.

It is for that reason that I am telling my story, for I

want the world to know that people like me who have returned from the half-world of mental oblivion are not forever contaminated. We have been sick. The best way to help us get well and stay well is to treat us like human beings — as I've been treated. We don't have to talk about our sickness in whispers or prowl about on the edge of society with our hands to our ears to block out the whispers of others. We have nothing to be ashamed of. All we want is to be understood by those who have never been where we have. There is no better therapy than understanding. I have received my share of that, for which I thank God every day of my life. But in order that I and others like me may be fully understood, I must tell my story from the beginning, for the source of my sickness goes far back beyond the day I blacked out in Sarasota.

I WAS born in Waterbury, Connecticut, on November 14, 1929. My parents were already well along in middle age. I had one brother, but, since he was nearly 20 years older than I, he belonged to another generation. He never was a factor in my life. He married while I was very young, and died a few years later. To all intents and purposes, I was brought up as an only child.

My dad was a house painter. When he worked, he made a good living, but he was idle much of the time. I don't remember his ever being very far ahead of the

[5]

world financially. At the time I was born, the great depression of the thirties was about to begin, and Waterbury was terribly badly hit. There were few jobs for anyone in those days, and practically no demand whatever for house painters.

One of my first memories was of my dad coming into the house, setting a huge bundle on the kitchen table and saying, "Well, we can be thankful for one thing. At least, we can get the bag."

I didn't know it then, but I found out later that "the bag" was the only thing that stood between us and starvation. It was a handout of food, given to the unemployed by the city of Waterbury once a week. It consisted mostly of canned goods and dry groceries, a little meat and fish and a few vegetables. It was supposed to last a week, but my mom had to do a lot of stretching to make it go that far. I was too young to realize it, for I was only three or four then, but there were a lot of hours near the tag end of the week when I cried from sheer hunger.

We lived in the back part of a wooden building at 683 East Main Street, in the heart of a working-class district. My parents still live there, and whenever I go to visit them I feel a pang of nostalgia, for, whether I liked it or not, it was home to me for nearly twenty years. I knew poverty, unhappiness, fear, even terror there, but there were good times, too, times when I knew real contentment and enjoyed good companionship and was the object of deep affection. When I walk into my old room on the second floor — that's my dad's room now — I can stifle the bad and lose myself in happy recollections of the good. There on the walls are the pictures of sports teams I played on while I was growing up. I never tire of looking at them, picking out old teammates and thinking of them as they are today. There, all about the room, are some of the things I made in school — the two flower-pot holders, the sewing basket I made for Mom, the two nightstands, the little bookcase, the smoking stand I made for my dad. In spite of everything, my modern home, my loyal wife, my wonderful family, my success in baseball, my strides toward financial security, my complete happiness in the life I now lead, the little wave of homesickness stops me for a minute or two each time I visit the apartment in Waterbury.

It had a good back yard and enough room for us all, but it wasn't much otherwise. Two brothers who owned the building lived in the front part. One was a tailor, the other a barber. Their shops were side by side, facing East Main Street. The entrance to our apartment was on one side. We had the entire rear of the building. The sitting room was downstairs, along with the kitchen and the bathroom. We had a coal stove, an icebox, two set tubs, a table and some chairs in the kitchen. There was a divan in the sitting room, along with a dining-room set, consisting of a table and four chairs, although we rarely ate there. Upstairs were two bedrooms and a big storage closet. In winter, my room was always ice cold, but I didn't mind. I slept well, and never suffered from anything in the way of colds more serious than occasional sniffles. To this day, I sleep with my bedroom windows wide open, regardless of the temperature outside.

We had no running hot water. When I took a bath, my mom would heat water on the stove and pour it into the tub for me. I never had a hot-water shower until I was old enough to take one at the school gymnasium. I have never lost my appreciation for one either. When I take a hot shower today, I stand under it as long as possible, enjoying every drop as it pours down over my body. A shower was the height of luxury for so many years that, to my dying day, I'll never take one for granted.

The back yard, which ran the width of the house, was fairly deep, and enclosed by a wooden fence. There were trees along one side and a tool shed on the other. Behind the shed, we kept three or four trash cans. In spite of these obstacles, there was enough room back there for my father and me to play catch. He was rolling a ball at me while I was still an infant, and tossing one at me when I was old enough to stand on my feet. One of my earliest memories — I couldn't have been more than four years old — was standing in the yard behind the house, catching a rubber ball and lobbing it back to my dad. I learned how to catch and throw a ball before I learned the alphabet.

I loved to catch a ball. It gave me a big thrill to snag it out of the air, especially when I had to stretch or reach around one of the back-yard obstacles. I used to ask my father to throw the ball high and to every corner of the yard, and if he didn't happen to be home, I'd do it for myself. When he wasn't around, I even practiced

catching a ball behind my back, although I didn't dare
let him catch me at it. It was only a stunt, and he would
say that stunts like that would serve no good purpose
during a real baseball game.

Once, when I was in the first grade, after I had made a
particularly hard catch in the back yard, I laughed and
said to my dad, "This is fun!"

"Of course it's fun," he agreed.

"But catching a ball," I said. "That's real fun."

He stopped and looked at me for a moment. Then he
said, slowly, "I don't want you thinking about fun. When
you grow up, I want you to become a slugger like Jimmy
Foxx. That's where the money is."

Jimmy Foxx was baseball's leading home-run hitter
at the time. He was my father's favorite ballplayer,
particularly since he had just been traded by the Philadelphia Athletics to the Boston Red Sox. The Red Sox
were my father's favorite team.

There were times when I loved my father and times
when whatever emotion I felt for him was anything but
love. I respected him, as I do today, but I was afraid of
him. Not a big man, he was stocky, with broad shoulders
and a flat stomach, and he had the strength of a bull.
When he was nice to me, he was as wonderful as any
father could be. He joked with me and bought me ice
cream and put his arm around me and sometimes even
kissed me. When he was like that, I felt very close to him.

But when he was angry, he terrified me. He used to
wear heavy shoes that tapered towards a point at the
toe. When I was a little slow getting ready to run an

errand, he would turn me around, let me go, then reach out with one foot and shove it in my direction, accompanying the gesture with a roaring, "Come on — get out!" If I didn't dodge fast enough, that sharp toe would land on my rump and I wouldn't be able to sit down for a week. When my dad was really angry, his sharp eyes would bore through me, his face and his gleaming bald head would redden and he would bellow at me in a voice that made the windows rattle and the pantry dishes jump. His voice was deep and raucous, and sometimes I could hear it in my sleep. I would do anything to avoid his anger. He set down my rules, and I tried hard not to disobey them, for I lived in fear of his wrath. I had to be home at five in the afternoon for supper and at seven-thirty in the evening for bed. When he wanted me, he whistled in a long, low, moaning whine. I got to dread that whistle, for it meant that time was short, and I rushed home the moment I heard it. There was a strapping waiting for me in case I was late.

My mom was gentle, sweet-faced and quiet. She had a soft, even voice, and when she was well she never raised it. When my father found fault with anything around the house, she let him roar himself out and then went about her business. At first, I used to think that his frequent outbursts of anger rolled off her back without leaving any effect, but later I learned better.

Whenever I got into trouble or did anything wrong, I went to my mother and told her everything.

"Do you want your dad to know?" she would ask.

"Does he *have* to know?" I'd reply.

Then we would talk it over. If it was obvious that he would find out sooner or later, I would agree to tell him myself. If there was a chance that we could keep it from him, she would agree not to say anything. There was nothing that I did wrong that my mom didn't know about. I loved her and trusted her, and she, in turn, showered me with affection.

I saw my first real baseball game when I was in kindergarten. There was an amateur league in Waterbury which played its games on Sundays at Hamilton Park, about a mile from my home. Overlooking the park was a high hill, which was generally known as "the mountain." You could see a ball game from there without paying your way into the park. My dad would take me over there, and we'd sit on the mountain and see the game.

"Watch closely," he said. "That's the only way you'll learn."

If I got restless or squirmed around, he would snap, "Quiet down and watch the ball game." But there was no question I could ask about the game that he wouldn't answer. He was impatient about a good many things, but never about my curiosity over baseball.

"You must learn baseball backwards and forwards," he told me. "The more you know, the better ballplayer you'll be."

I could tell what a batter should do in a given situation before I could write my name. By the time I was in the first grade, I was an ardent Red Sox fan. I listened to their games on the radio when I wasn't out playing ball, and I knew the names of everyone on the team. I grew up a Red Sox fan. It never occurred to me to cheer for anyone else, even though in Waterbury we were within radio range of the Braves, who were then also in Boston, the two New York teams, the Giants and the Yankees, and the Brooklyn Dodgers. My dad was strictly a Red Sox man. So was I.

When I was five years old, my parents entered me in the kindergarten of the Sacred Heart School, a parochial school operated by the Sacred Heart Church, which was on East Main Street, almost next door to my house. My father is a Protestant, but my mother, a devout Catholic, wanted me to be brought up in the Church, and my father had no objections.

I did not dislike school, although in common with all the other kids, I could think of a lot of things I'd rather do than go there. The nuns at Sacred Heart were gentle and understanding, and I could relax when I was with them. One of them became almost a second mother to me. Her name was Sister Margaret. She was my first-grade teacher.

The first time I ever had any direct contact with Sister Margaret was just before recess on my first day in her class. We were walking towards the school yard when I stepped out of line. Before I knew what was happening, she had swooped down on me and, gently pulling me by the ear, put me back where I belonged.

Later, while we were outside, she came over to me and said, softly, "You're Jimmy Piersall, aren't you?"

"Yes, Sister," I mumbled.

"I'm glad to see you, Jimmy. Your mother is my very dear friend."

"Thank you, Sister."

"You're a nice boy. And after this, you *will* keep in line, won't you?"

"Yes, Sister."

After a while, she began referring to me as "my Jimmy." If anyone asked for me, she would say, "My Jimmy's outside playing ball. I can hear his voice." Or, if I got into trouble and she heard about it, it would be, "That's too bad. I guess I'll have to go and pull my Jimmy's ear."

At first, she pulled my ear only when she was really displeased about something I did, but she never hurt me. As I grew older and we became closer, she began pulling my ear in jest, until it finally got to be a game with us. She does it now as a greeting whenever we meet.

I could talk to Sister Margaret the way I talked to my own mother. She knew my mother so very well and felt so close to her that we had our affection for Mom in common. By the time I was in the second grade, Sister Margaret developed into more than just a dear friend. She became the one stabilizing influence in my life, the only person I knew to whom I could pour out my problems and with whom I could relax completely. I came to love her as I loved my own mother because, in effect, that was exactly what she had to be to me.

One day, while I was in the second grade, I came home from school and found my father sitting on the divan downstairs, staring into space. He seemed deeply agitated, so I decided not to bother him. Instead, I went into the kitchen, looking for my mother. She was not there. I went to the foot of the stairs and called up to her, but she didn't answer. Then, alarmed, I looked back at my father. He was still sitting there, his brows knit in a frown, but he seemed to be more puzzled than angry. I couldn't tell for sure, but it looked a little as if he had been weeping.

"Where's Mom?" I asked.

"She's gone away," he said, shortly.

For a minute, I didn't get the full significance of it.

"Gone away?" I repeated aimlessly. "Where has she gone?"

"Away. Just away."

I stood and stared at him for a few seconds, my eyes filling, my lips quivering, my shoulders shaking. His face softened and, beckoning with his forefinger, he said quietly, "Come here, son."

I rushed across the room and collapsed, sobbing, in his arms. He talked to me, but I have no idea what he said, nor do I know how long we sat there. The first thing I remember is looking up at him and asking, "When will she be back?"

"Soon. She'll be back soon," my dad said.

"How soon?"

"A little while."

He set me down, then gently turning me so that I faced him, he said, "We'll take care of each other for now. I'll do the cooking and you'll do the dishes. We'll make our own beds and work together with the cleaning. And before you know it, your mom'll be home. Now how about a game of catch?"

We were very close that day, my dad and I, maybe closer than we've ever been before or since. We went into the back yard and played catch for hours, then, back in the house, he cooked dinner for us both. After he put me to bed, though, I lay and sobbed for a long time. I couldn't imagine what life would be like without my mom.

I told Sister Margaret the next day.

"My mom has gone away," I said, in a dull monotone.

"You'll see her soon," she remarked.

I looked sharply at her.

"Do you know where she is?"

"She's not very far away."

"Will she ever come home again?"

"Of *course* she will," Sister assured me.

When I got home after Mass on the following Sunday, my dad, dressed in his best suit, was waiting for me in front of the house. Parked on the street, the sun's rays dancing over its shining top, was the car he had bought during a period of prosperity a few months before. My father was very proud of that car. Every Sunday he spent hours polishing it, and he wiped it clean of the day's accumulation of dirt every evening.

He was smiling broadly.

"Get in, son," he said, jovially. "We're going for a ride."

"Where?"

"To see your mother."

"Mom?"

I couldn't say more. Without another word I got into the car, and Dad, after making sure the door was shut securely, walked around and climbed into the driver's seat.

An hour later, we pulled into the grounds of what looked to me like an exclusive private school. It was a pleasant spring afternoon, and the wide expanses of grass were already a rich sea green. There was a sign leading into the driveway, but we were going too fast for me to read it. I didn't know it then, but for the next ten years I would have plenty of chance to spell out the words. They read, "Norwich State Hospital."

Mom seemed perfectly all right to me. She cried a little as she embraced me, then sat with us and talked for an hour or so. She asked me about school and baseball and church and Sister Margaret, and I told her everything I could. She and Dad talked quietly, except for one or two occasions when he raised his voice a little. Dad and Mom never could talk quietly together for any length of time.

"When will you be home?" I asked, just before we left.

"After I've had a good rest," she replied. "It won't be long. And Jim —"

"Yes?"

"Take good care of your father."

"I will, Mom."

She was home six months or so later, and our threads

of life, on the surface, at least, seemed to pick up where they had been left off. But it wasn't the same. Mom, usually so calm and steady, didn't move around the house with the quiet dignity of the old days. Sometimes she worked fast as she did the household chores, as if she couldn't wait to get them over with. She was nervous and fidgety, and she did things in quick, jerky movements. And when she talked, her voice rose occasionally, although she talked little. Every so often I caught her shuddering convulsively.

Then, a year later, disaster struck again. It was just before my ninth birthday, and I was coming home from school. As I approached the house, I could hear my parents arguing, my father's booming voice raised in the anger that I dreaded, my mother's querulous and shrill. As I turned from the street into the path that led to our entrance on the side, I nearly collided with my dad, who was rushing out. I stepped aside and he brushed past me without a word.

Mom was in the kitchen, sobbing hysterically. I tried to put my arm around her, but she shoved me aside.

"I've got to get away from here," she kept repeating. "I can't stand it."

She said it louder and louder, while I stood by, frightened, worried and unable to do anything to quiet her down.

Then, suddenly, she stood up, crossed the room and headed down the steps. I jumped up and followed her, but she was on the path before I had reached the door. When I got outside, she was walking rapidly towards the street, where, as usual, trucks and buses were roaring back and forth, in and out of town. Before I knew it, Mom was stepping off the curb, and, to my horror, slowing up to a deliberate shuffle. Oblivious to the traffic, she looked neither to the right nor the left as she started to cross the street.

For a moment I froze where I stood. Miraculously, she didn't get hit, although swearing, sweating drivers had to jam on brakes and swerve to one side or another to keep from running into her. She was more than halfway across before I realized what she was trying to do. I dashed madly after her, and, without bothering to look at the traffic myself, rushed up behind her and pushed her the rest of the way across. Then, after waiting for a break in the traffic, we crossed back to our own side together and went into the house.

We both cried for a long time. Then Mom, calm and lucid, said, "Jim, I'm going away again."

"To — that place?"

"Yes. Don't worry about me. I'll be back."

My dad and I saw her at Norwich two Sundays later. She seemed normal and made it evident that she was glad to see us. After I kissed her, I said, "Mom, get well and come home soon. Dad's not a very good cook and I'm not a very good bed maker."

She smiled, and assured me that she'd be back sometime, but she didn't say when. We stayed with her for a while, and then drove home in silence.

After I went to bed that night, I tossed restlessly back and forth, thinking of my mother and wondering why I couldn't have her with me all the time, the way other kids had their mothers. The more I thought about it, the sorrier I felt for myself, and I finally broke into a fit of hysterical sobbing. I cried and cried until, at last, my father came in and said, "What's the matter, son?"

I sat up in bed, pointing at him and screamed, "You know what the matter is. I don't want my mom in that awful place any more. I can't stand it. I want her home, where she belongs. If you'd stop hollering at her all the time, she'd be all right. You haven't got any patience with her. You're always yelling at her. If you didn't then she wouldn't have to go away."

My father didn't move. He looked down at me a long time, then said, quietly, "Son, you don't understand her the way I do. And you don't understand me, either."

He came over and sat on the edge of the bed.

"Did I ever tell you about my own childhood?" he asked.

I had stopped crying, and, as I looked up at him, I realized that I had never heard him mention his own people. Not speaking, I simply shook my head.

"Well," he said, "I guess you might say I never had any childhood. I certainly didn't have any home life. I never knew either of my parents. My father left home and my mother died while I was still a baby. Can you imagine what that means, son?"

I could only shake my head again.

"It means that nobody — *nobody*" — his voice was harsh now — "gives a rap whether you live or you die. I love you. Your mom loves you. You have teachers who help you and friends who want to play with you. I had nobody, I tell you. *Not one person!*"

His voice was rising, but this time I wasn't frightened. I simply sat and stared at him.

"They put me in a foster home. The State of Connecticut paid for my keep. The people I lived with covered the law. They clothed me and fed me and provided me with a bed to sleep in. But they didn't give me the one thing I needed more than anything — affection. I didn't know what the word meant, but I knew that other kids had it. But other kids lived with their own parents, who loved them. I lived with strangers.

"I couldn't stand it, not loving anyone, not having anyone to love me. One day — I was younger than you are now — I ran away. I scrounged and scrambled for a living, moving from place to place, existing from day to day, hungering for something that wasn't for me.

"I had to fight to live," he said, his eyes glowing in the semidarkness. "It was a dog-eat-dog existence. The older I got, the more I realized that if I wanted anything done for myself, I'd have to do it myself or it wouldn't get done. And if I wanted anything, I'd have to demand it — in as loud a voice as possible."

He stopped a minute and took a deep breath.

"I don't mean to yell at people — you, your mom, anyone. I just can't help myself. You can't blame me. I *had* to do it for so many years —"

Then he turned and walked out, gently closing my bedroom door behind him.

When I saw Sister Margaret at school the next day, I

[20]

asked her, "Why does my mother have to keep going to the hospital all the time?"

"Because she has to rest."

"I know, Sister. But *why* does she have to rest?"

"She tires easily, Jimmy. And she has to work hard."

I looked at Sister for a long moment. Her face was composed, her eyes clear and calm, her lips parted in a half-smile as she gazed back at me. She seemed so strong and solid and dependable that I was sure she would have a satisfactory answer for anything I asked her.

"Sister," I said slowly, "why does God punish my mom? Why does He make her keep going to that place? Why does He let her get so nervous and upset and unhappy? She's a good lady, Sister. She's charitable. She goes to church. She obeys all the laws. She works hard. She always does her best. *Sister, what has my mom done wrong that these awful things have to happen to her?*"

"She's done nothing wrong, Jimmy. And God isn't punishing her. Everyone has a cross to bear. Hers is this sickness. She has a fear she can't express, and it has made her sick."

I was barely nine years old. I felt that I was neither old enough nor smart enough to understand.

It was two years now since my mom first got sick. During that time, I had never known a moment when I didn't worry about her. When she was away, I worried how long she'd be gone. When she was home, I worried how long it would be before she would have to go away again. Each day she was with us, I left the house with the gnawing fear that she might not be there when I got back. I was afraid to go to school, and afraid to walk into the house after I got out.

Even at nine, I was a bundle of nerves. The constant apprehension about Mom was only the beginning. I worried about everything. I worried about school and about my playmates liking me and about what we were going to have for dinner and about how my dad would be feeling when I got home. Each June I worried about getting promoted and each September I worried about my new teacher.

The older I got, the more I worried. When I was in the sixth grade, I made the Sacred Heart baseball team. I was the youngest boy on the club, but I was the best fielder in school, and Bobby Ray, the coach, put me in center field. I couldn't wait to play every day, and if something came up to prevent our practicing or having a game, I was bitterly disappointed. One day, we couldn't practice because we didn't have a ball.

"We won't let this happen again," said Bobby. "From now on, each boy will contribute a dime and that will give us enough to buy a ball."

The kids went home for money, and we chipped in enough for a ball. But after that, I took it upon myself to make sure we had one. I was the one who always collected the money and bought the ball because I was afraid nobody else would do it, and then we wouldn't be able to play. I was always worried about not being able to have a game. If the weather was threatening when I got up in the morning, I fretted all through school, worrying about rain. If a sudden storm came up while we were playing, I huddled in a corner and prayed that it would stop.

I got to be a long-distance worrier as well as a short-term worrier. I worried just as much about what might happen in ten years as I did about what might happen in two hours. Outside of the everlasting worry about my mom, my biggest concern was whether or not I'd ever be big enough or good enough to play major-league base-ball. My father had put the idea in my head, but it be-came the one burning ambition of my life. I was just as anxious to make it as he was to see me do it.

His praise meant more than anything else to me. The first time he ever saw me play in a game, I rushed over to him after it was over and said, a little breathlessly, "Dad, did I do all right?"

"I think you did fine, son," he answered in his gruff voice. "You made mistakes, but you'll always make mistakes. Even big leaguers do that. Nobody ever plays the game perfectly."

That was enough for me. My dad was satisfied that I had done all right. As we walked home together, I was proud and happy. His standards were strict, and I had measured up to them. Nothing was more important to me than that.

BACK when I was about seven, the milkman on our route had said to me one morning, "How would you like to give me a hand delivering milk? I'll pay you thirty cents a day. All you have to do is work an hour and a half every morning before school."

I asked my father that evening if it would be all right.

"We get along," he said. "You don't have to work. You're too young. Besides, I want you free to play baseball."

"Please, Dad," I said. "It will only be in the morning. I'll give you the money and you can save it for me."

"Well — all right. I'll put it aside for your school clothes."

That was my first job. I got up at six-fifteen in the morning and met the milkman in front of the house half an hour later. I worked until quarter past eight, delivering milk in the neighborhood, then went to school. The thirty cents I got every day looked like a lot of money to me. I gave it to my dad at night, and he put it away for me.

Later in the year, I had a chance to get a Saturday job delivering groceries for a market down the street. When I asked my dad about it, he said, "You can take it, but be sure to tell them you can work all day only during the winter. Come spring, you're going to play baseball in the afternoon."

"Can I work mornings in the spring?"

"That's all right. But not afternoons."

I worked in the market for several years. When I was about ten, Jimmy Phelan, manager of the meat department, said, "Jimmy, we're going to need help around Thanksgiving time. How would you like to learn to clean turkeys? I'll give you a nickel for every one you do."

In the two days before Thanksgiving, I dressed one hundred turkeys and made five dollars. The only trouble was, the paring knife was sharp and not easy to handle. It slipped every so often, and I gave myself some nasty cuts. But I didn't dare let my father see them, so I used to put on a little gauze and adhesive tape and tell him they were scratches. Fortunately, although some of the cuts were deep, none was very long. I still carry scars on my hands from them.

Dad was always warning me about being careful of hand or arm injuries.

"You have a good, strong throwing arm," he said. "You can't afford to have anything happen to it. In baseball, you need good arms as well as good legs. And be careful of your fingers. You can't have anything happen to them, or it might affect your hitting. Remember, son, you grip a bat with all ten fingers. If anything's wrong with one of them, it can ruin you."

Every job I ever had was determined by whether or not it would take time away from baseball. There was a gas station across the street from us, and behind it was a big empty lot where some of the older boys played ball afternoons. I used to go over there all the time to play with them. One day I was offered a job pumping gas a couple of hours Saturday evenings. I was about ten years old then. I worked there Saturday nights for years because it didn't interfere with baseball. The only Saturdays I missed were when I played basketball in high school and we had Saturday night games. I get lonesome for the gas station whenever I think of Waterbury. It's now run by a couple of young war veterans, Howie Gilland and Charley Martone. I still go over and help them pump gas for an hour or two whenever I go to Waterbury.

My dad let me take over a paper route when I was in the fifth grade. I paid eleven dollars to the boy who had it before me. It included deliveries in my immediate neighborhood and the rights to sell papers in front of the Sacred Heart Church on Sundays. Since I made good money and there was no time taken away from baseball, it was an ideal job.

On weekday mornings I didn't have to work as long as I had for the milkman and I made much more money. By eight o'clock I was all through. My Sunday-morning schedule was busy, but worthwhile. I used to get up at quarter of five and go across the street to a little variety store, where my papers were left for me. I'd count them out, leave them there, go to five-thirty Mass, come out at six, pick up my papers, make my deliveries between Masses and be back in front of the church by seven o'clock. I'd be sold out by ten. I could make twelve dollars a Sunday and still have most of the day free for baseball. I sold papers until I started playing high-school basketball. After those Saturday-night games, I couldn't get up early Sundays. I sold the daily route for fifteen dollars and got twenty-five for the Sunday route and the church location.

Basketball was the only game other than baseball that my father would let me play. It was the big winter sport around Waterbury, so it served as a good outlet while I was waiting for the baseball season to roll around. My closest friend, Bernie Sherwill, a short, dark-haired boy, was a fine basketball player and he wanted me to go out for the high-school team with him. My father gave me permission, and basketball became the secondary sports love of my life.

I decided to go to Leavenworth High, a public school, instead of to a parochial high school. The reason was that it would give me more time for baseball, since the high-school kids got out earlier than the parochial-school kids. The switch from Sacred Heart to Leavenworth was my idea, and my father enthusiastically endorsed it.

Bernie is still the best friend I have. Outside of a few neighbors and family friends he was the only boy my age who knew about my mother. When I realized that she suffered from mental illness, I was careful to hide it from most people, but I told Bernie all about it. I was in the eighth grade by this time, and I was desperately anxious for Bernie to understand me. At that point, I needed a lot of understanding.

I couldn't stay still longer than a few minutes at a time. I didn't know how to pace myself. I had to be on the go all the time. It was impossible for me to read a book because that meant being in one place too long. I couldn't sit through a movie. I was unable to concentrate on anything except when I was actually playing baseball or basketball. I had to have constant action, and my worst hours came when I had nothing to do. I was a perpetual-motion machine, always wound up like a spring and never able to uncoil completely. No matter what I did or how exhausted I became doing it, I had to keep going. I might run dry physically, but my nerves kept pushing me to do more. I drew on every ounce of my reserve every day. All of my blood, my guts, my flesh and my physical and mental capacities were poured indiscriminately into everything. I couldn't stop the mad merry-go-round of activity. Worse, I couldn't figure out what it was that kept driving me.

"Take it easy, Jim," Bernie said. "There's plenty of time."

"I know. But I have to get things done," I answered.

"Why?"

"I just do, that's all."

"So you'll have more time to loaf?" he asked.

"No. So I can get to the next thing I have to do."

"Relax. Nothing's that important."

But *everything* was that important. Bernie didn't agree with me and he didn't know what made me tick, but he *did* understand that I couldn't help myself. More than once, he had to defend me when the other kids objected to the way I talked and acted.

No matter what I was doing, I couldn't keep from yelling instructions to the other guys. During baseball games, especially, I was always shrieking at the top of my lungs, telling everyone else what to do. I not only worried about myself, but I worried about the whole team. I played center field, and I tried to run everything from out there. I yelled to the other fielders where to play opposing hitters, and I yelled to the pitcher what to throw, and I yelled to the umpire what to call. When we were at bat, I yelled to our own hitters, and when I was up myself, I yelled to the base runners, if any, or the coaches.

When I played basketball, I yelled instructions from the minute the game started until the minute it ended. In huddles, when there was time out, I was always the one who did the talking. During the football season I yelled from the sidelines. My father flatly refused to let me play football, which I loved, but I held the first-down stakes during the games, and that brought me close to the action. I yelled as much from there as I did from my positions in the other sports.

Every night I came home hoarse and exhausted. From my sophomore year in high school on, I couldn't even unwind at night. I had to replay every move of every game, whether I had taken part in it or not. I did it over and over. It took hours for me to fall asleep, but when I succeeded, I slept soundly enough. Every morning I bounced out of bed, eager to get back on the merry-go-round. No matter how much of myself I had squeezed out one day, I always seemed to have a rich new supply to squeeze out the next.

One morning when I was about fifteen years old, I woke up with a terrific headache. It was the day after a tough basketball game which had left me in a turmoil. I had tossed and turned most of the night and had slept only a few hours. I felt as if a steel band was drawn tightly across my forehead, which throbbed with pain. I climbed out of bed and bathed my face in ice-cold water. That gave me some relief. The pains were no longer intense, and after a while they nearly subsided altogether. But every day after that I woke up with a headache, and it stayed with me in some form or other almost all the time. Sometimes the pain was acute, as it had been that first morning. Most of the time, I was aware only of a dull ache that occasionally throbbed a little.

At first I thought I had a sinus condition, but then I noticed the headaches were worse after I had been yelling a lot. I began telling myself to quiet down, and I would start a day determined to let nature take its course in the afternoon's game, but that did no good. I had to keep taking charge of everything. The headaches persisted, and after a while I came to accept them as part of my daily existence. They annoyed me and I wished they would go away, but I didn't do anything about them. I simply suffered them in silence, and sometimes I almost managed to ignore them.

I rarely mentioned them to anyone. But one morning I couldn't get up, and when my dad came into my room to see what was wrong, I said, "I've got a sinus headache."

"Does it bother you so much that you can't get up?" he asked.

"It's pretty bad, Dad."

"O.K. Stay home from school. I'll get you some aspirin before I leave to go to work. Better stay in bed. You'll be all right tomorrow."

I stayed in bed, but I wasn't much better the next morning. I didn't tell my father that. I managed to struggle out of bed and go to school, and he thought I had fully recovered. I didn't dare tell him the headaches occurred so often, because I was afraid he would make me go to see a doctor. Then I might have to rest, or, at least, stay away from sports for a while, and I couldn't stand that.

I wished I could take the games more in stride. Every game, whether it was basketball or baseball, seemed to mean everything to me. When a close decision went against us, I rushed to the official who called it and argued for long minutes with him, even though I realized as often as not that I was the one who was wrong. When we won I felt good, but I was desolate when we lost. Invariably, after a losing game, I slept worse and woke up with a more severe headache than usual.

Before each game, Bernie and I would go to church and light candles to the Blessed Mother.

"Please," I would pray, "don't let me argue with the officials. Please let me keep my temper. And please, *please,* let us win so I won't be upset."

In high school, I had a new idol. He was Bill Tracy, the football, baseball and basketball coach. Bill was six feet tall and a graduate of Villanova College, where he had been an all-round athlete. He was a serious man, with a slow smile, and he spoke in a gentle voice. He suffered terribly from hay fever. During the pollen season, he could hardly breathe, and I used to hold my own breath when he had a spasm and pray inwardly that he'd get some relief.

He was strict, but fair. All of the boys started from scratch with him and he made us feel that we had really earned something whenever we made one of his teams.

He knew more about me than I thought he did, as I found out when I tried to go out for football in my sophomore year. It was the first time I ever willfully disobeyed my father. I knew he didn't want me to play because he was afraid I would get hurt badly enough to ruin my baseball career, but I loved the game and was sure that I could protect myself. I figured that if I did make the team, he'd be so proud that he'd let me play anyhow.

But Bill Tracy never gave me a chance to find out whether I could make the team or not. When he saw me among the other football candidates he pulled me aside and said, "Jim, I'm not going to give you a suit."

"Why?" I asked, innocently.

"You know why. Your father doesn't want you to play."

"Let me try, Coach. I'm sure he'll let me go through with it if I make the team."

"No, Jim. He made a special point of talking to me about it and I promised him I wouldn't let you play. Your father wants you to be a big-league ballplayer, and he doesn't intend to let anything happen that might prevent it. If you ruin yourself for baseball by suffering a serious football injury, I'd never forgive myself."

I turned away, so obviously disappointed that Bill stopped me and said, kindly, "You can hold the first-down stakes during games. You can't get any closer than that without playing."

I was at the football field every day, and I held the stakes at both the varsity and the junior-varsity games. The two teams were practically interchangeable, since Tracy and his assistant, "Jarp" O'Neil, worked with both. The two squads would practice together, and in the early weeks of the season, Bill would pick the varsity out of the whole group the day before the games. The junior varsity had its own schedule.

Bill's father died, and the funeral was held on the day of a junior-varsity game. Jarp was left in charge that afternoon and I went to work on him.

"How about letting me play?" I said.

"You can't play, Jim. You're not allowed to."

"Just this once, Jarp. What's the difference? Bill won't mind."

"I can't let you play," he insisted. "What if you got hurt? I'd probably get fired and your dad would never forgive either of us."

"Oh, Jarp, I won't get hurt. You can use a good end, can't you? And have you got a guy who can punt as well as I can?"

"Well — I don't know."

He was softening up. I knew he didn't have a punter, and I could kick the ball well. And the junior-varsity ends were weak. I was faster and could catch passes better than anyone on the whole squad, let alone just the J.V.'s.

"This one game?" I said, softly. "Bill'll be back tomor-

[33]

row and I'll never get another chance. Please, Jarp?"

"Oh, all right. Only, for the love of Mike, be careful. We'll both get murdered if anything happens to you."

I played and had a field day. I caught half a dozen passes, did all of the kicking and either scored or made the key plays that led to all our touchdowns. The climax came in the last period, when I intercepted a pass behind our own goal line and ran 102 yards for a touchdown. We won the game, and when it was over, Jarp rushed over to me, whacked me on the back and yelled, "Jim, you were great. And you didn't get a scratch!"

I was in a schoolboy's seventh heaven. I had always felt that I could play football well enough to make the team, but this was the first chance I had ever had to prove it. I felt wonderful showering and dressing after the game, and I was walking on air when I left for home.

But by the time I got there, my feet were like lead. On the way I suddenly realized that it would be impossible to keep my father from knowing that I'd played. The Waterbury sports pages would carry the story of the game and so would the sports announcers on the radio. There wasn't any question about who would get most of the credit for winning the game. If I'd had a name like Smith or Jones, I might have bluffed it through, but the only other Piersall in Waterbury was my dad. He'd know what had happened the minute he turned on the radio.

I rushed into the house, and my father was in the kitchen, getting dinner ready. I could tell by his greeting that he hadn't heard anything yet.

"How are you, Dad?"

"Fine, son. Have a good day?"

"Fine. Say, dad — uh — before you listen to a sports program on the radio or pick up the paper, I've got something to tell you."

"What?" he asked indifferently. He was leaning over the stove, stirring a stew.

"I played football today."

His body stiffened and the spoon in his hand froze. For a few seconds he remained in the position I'd found him in, leaning over the stove. Then he straightened up, whirled around and, brandishing the spoon, roared, "You *what?*"

"It was only with the J.V.'s, Dad," I said, the words tumbling on top of each other. "You can't get hurt playing J.V. football. I never heard of anyone getting hurt in a J.V. game. And, Dad, I was the star of the game. I caught a flock of passes and I intercepted one and ran one hundred and two yards for a touchdown."

Measuring each word, my father said, tightly, "What — was — that — Bill — Tracy — thinking — of? He gave me his word —"

"Bill Tracy wasn't there, Dad."

"Then who gave you permission to play?" he thundered.

"Nobody — really. It was my fault. I talked Jarp O'Neil into letting me play. He couldn't refuse. I nagged him and nagged him. Dad, look. I'm all right. I didn't even break a fingernail. And did you hear what I did? I ran one hundred and two yards for a touchdown."

[35]

"You did, eh?"

"Yes, and we won the game. I won it."

"Is that so?"

He lowered the spoon, and looked searchingly at me. Then, his voice normal, he said, "Well now, that's fine. I'm glad you got it all out of your system. But, son, don't you *ever* — do you hear me? — *don't you ever again play football.* Do you understand?"

"Yes, Dad. I understand."

Then he turned around, leaned over the stove and started stirring the stew again.

When Bernie and I first reported for varsity basketball during our sophomore year, I had little hopes of making the team. There were some good boys at Leavenworth High, and the competition for positions would be keen. Bill Tracy was not the kind of coach who made up his mind in a hurry. He wanted to see everyone in action, not once but several times, before deciding whom to put on the squad.

I was terribly anxious to make it, and actually good enough to make it, but I was utterly devoid of self-confidence. It seemed to me that a dozen guys were better than I on the basketball floor, and no matter what I did, I couldn't make myself believe that I had a chance. The coach was completely impartial. Right up to the last minute he gave no indication of which of the sophomores would go along.

On the day before the team was to leave for Ansonia to open the season, I said to Bernie, "Well, I hope you win Saturday."

"What do you mean, *you* hope *we* win?" he snapped. "You got other plans or something?"

"I won't make it. I'm not good enough."

"You're only about as good as anyone on the club, and better than most. What's the matter with you, Jim? Of course you'll make it."

I didn't agree with him. I was so sure I wouldn't go with the team that I didn't even bother to tell my father when the boys were leaving. But I lay awake most of the night, worrying about my chances, and went to school the next morning with chills of anticipation running up and down my spine.

When afternoon practice was over Tracy read off the names of the guys who were going to Ansonia and I was on the list.

"All right, boys," he announced. "I'll see you at the station tonight. The train leaves at seven o'clock."

That gave me a couple of hours to get home and pack before meeting the team. But I couldn't wait two hours. I couldn't wait ten minutes. I ran most of the way home. I had to tell my dad. He was a hot basketball fan. It was the only sport that could, in its own season, get his mind a little bit off baseball.

But the door was locked when I got home. Mom was away, and, after I tried to get in, I remembered that Dad had mentioned something about getting home late because he was hoping to finish a job that day. He might be home any minute — or he might not be home for hours.

With a deep, sinking sensation in the pit of my stom-

[37]

ach, I made a tour of the windows. Sometimes, one would be open or, at least, unlocked, and I could get in that way. I didn't have much hope, though, because my father was always very thorough about things like that. He checked everything before going out. He left a window unlocked if I asked him to, but only when there was no question that I would get home before he did.

First, I tried to be calm about the situation. I pulled at the door, then went to each window, trying to convince myself that one would be open. But then, when I realized that I was locked out and that precious time was being wasted, the sinking sensation exploded into panic. Frantically I rushed around and around, yanking and heaving at one window after another, tugging at the door, alternately trying one, then the other. Upset as I was, I didn't dare break a window. That would have infuriated my father.

By now, I was conscious of nothing except the passing of the minutes and the certainty of impending disaster. *If I couldn't get into the house, I couldn't go to Ansonia. And if I couldn't go to Ansonia, I couldn't play in the game. I'd be letting the whole team down. What would the other kids say? What would Bill Tracy say? He wouldn't stand for my missing the train. He'd fire me right off the team.*

I lost track of the time while I literally ran around in circles endlessly trying door and windows as if, by force of will, I could get something to give. It was a hopeless situation. It took me a long while to realize it. When at last I did, I sat down on the stoop and wept.

[38]

I don't know how long I sat there, crying my eyes out and wishing I were dead, but when I finally looked at my watch, it was after seven, and the train was gone. *There was nothing I could do now to save the situation. As far as Leavenworth High was concerned, I was ruined. Bill Tracy was the baseball coach, too. He'd never trust me again.*

After a while, still crying, I stood up, and half-blindly started down the street. My father hadn't come home yet, so I headed for Artie Barstis's house. He lived on East Main, on the other side of the street and about a block away from me with his brother, his sister Judy, and her husband. I had known them all my life, and the family had always been nice to me. When I walked into the house, Judy was home alone, ironing.

She heard me sobbing and, turning towards me, said, "For heaven's sake, Jim, what's wrong?"

"I can't get into the house," I blubbered. "The train's already left. What can I do? I'll lose my job."

"What train? What job? Now, Jim, you're a big boy. Stop crying. Things can't be that bad."

"They can't be any worse."

She put her arms on my shoulders and pushed me over to a chair.

"All right," she said. "Calm down, and tell me what happened."

"I made the basketball team today," I finally managed to say.

"Well, that's wonderful."

"It *was* wonderful. It isn't wonderful any more. I was

[39]

supposed to be at the station at seven o'clock to go to Ansonia, but I couldn't get in the house, so I missed the train. Now I'll lose my job. Tracy'll never understand. He doesn't know how things are at my house. Gee, Judy, you don't know how hard I worked to get that job. And now I've lost it."

I started to sob again.

"Don't cry," Judy said. "I'm sure Tracy will understand. You just tell him what happened. And if you worked that hard, you'll get your job back. Don't worry."

Dad was heartbroken when he got home and found out what happened.

"Why didn't you tell me?" he asked.

"Because I didn't think I'd make the team."

"Well, after this, I'll leave the key in the shed or something. We can't have this happen again."

I *did* lose my job, but only for one game. Even then, Tracy pulled me aside and said, kindly, "Don't worry, Jim. I understand. You'll be back."

From then on, I never had a problem I didn't take to Bill Tracy. To this day, he's my most trusted adviser and one of the closest friends I have in the world.

W HILE I confined all my basketball to the school team, I played baseball wherever I could. We had a good city league in Waterbury, and I made the Franco-American team when I was sixteen years old. We won the State title the next year and played in the Eastern championships at Baltimore. I still wasn't as big as I wanted to be, although I was learning to hit. But my batting had always been far behind my fielding. I could handle a ball that came anywhere near me, and I often made catches that seemed close to impossible. I was desperately unsure of myself in everything else I did, but I had absolute confidence in my ability to catch a fly ball, once it left a hitter's bat. I never went after one that I wasn't positive I was going to get, and I was surprised and unhappy if the ball fell out of my reach. My arm was getting stronger all the time, too. I could throw hard, and threw to the right base almost by instinct.

Waterbury, halfway between Boston and New York, was literally crawling with big-league baseball scouts. All of the sixteen major-league clubs had men covering Connecticut, and they converged on Waterbury from time to time. Since baseball rules prohibit the signing of a schoolboy until his high-school class has graduated, I was never directly approached until my senior year, but scouts were sounding out Bill Tracy and my dad long before that.

During the late fall of 1946, just after I had become a senior at Leavenworth High, Dad said one day, "I want you to go to college."

"College? Me? Who's going to pay for it?" I demanded.

"Wouldn't you like to go to college, son?"

"Like it? Holy cow! I'd love it! It'd be wonderful to go to college. But — it's impossible!"

"Well," my dad said, calmly, "you're going."

I couldn't believe my ears. The only boys I knew who

ever got to college were guys who had won football scholarships or had returned from the service and were getting their tuition paid under the G.I. bill. I didn't fit into either category, and I told my father so.

"You don't have to fit into either category," Dad said. "You're going to Duke University."

"Duke?" I repeated, stupidly.

"That's right. Duke gives baseball scholarships. Jack Coombs, the old Philadelphia Athletics pitcher, is the baseball coach there. He's one of the finest in the business. He's going to teach you a lot of baseball, son."

"Why — sure. That's fine. That's great. Only what makes you think I can get one of those scholarships?"

"You're going to be offered one next spring. And you're going to take it."

"I thought you were so anxious for me to play ball."

"I am. I intend for you to play ball. But you'll only be seventeen when you get out of high school. You'll be too young to play professional ball. Besides, I *want* you to go to college. You can sign a contract when you graduate."

He smiled. Then, his gruff voice toned down almost to a whisper, he mused, "Imagine. A son of mine a college man!" Then he glared at me and snapped, "You'd better stay in shape. Don't do anything foolish."

"Don't worry, Dad. I won't."

Two weeks later, I broke my right wrist when I fell on it chasing a forward pass during a touch-football game at the Y.M.C.A. playground. I knew it was broken the minute I hit the ground, because I could hear the bone crack.

Ed Readell, the "Y" recreational director, helped me up, then said, "Come on, Jim. We'll get that set quick."

"It's broken, isn't it?"

I was talking almost automatically. The pain was intense, but that didn't bother me. *What would my dad say? What if the arm didn't knit properly? What if I couldn't throw hard any more? What if I couldn't hold a bat? How could I face my father with a broken right wrist? Why, I might not even be able to play basketball! And the season was only three weeks away.*

Ed stayed with me while the doctor set my wrist.

"Is it bad, Doc?" I asked.

"It's a good, clean break," he replied.

"Will it knit right?"

"It should. Ought to be stronger than ever when it does."

"When will it be O.K. again?"

"Oh, five-six weeks. We'll take the cast off in about three."

"Can't you take it off earlier?" I pleaded.

"Why?"

"So I can play basketball. The season starts in three weeks."

Bernie Sherwill and I were co-captains of the school basketball team. We had a fine team coming up — maybe even a championship team.

"Doc, I've *got* to be ready to play basketball."

"We'll see," he said. That was as far as he would go.

Outside, Readell asked, "Can you get home all right?"

"Please, Ed. Do me a favor? Come home with me — just for a few minutes?"

"Why, sure — if you want me to."

I couldn't face my father alone. On the way to our house, I said, "Tell my dad the doctor said my arm will be all right. Tell him I'll be able to play basketball — and baseball. Tell him what the doctor said — that I'll be stronger than ever. And tell him it wasn't my fault I got hurt."

I made Ed go in ahead of me. Dad was in the kitchen when we walked in. Before Ed could say anything, he saw the cast on my arm. Without a word, he sat down heavily, cradled his head in his arms and cried like a baby. Then he looked up and sobbed, "After all I tried to do to keep you for baseball, look what you did to yourself. Now everything's gone — basketball, baseball, college, the big leagues — everything."

It took us half an hour to calm him down and another half hour to convince him that it was only a routine break, with no complications. By the time Ed got up to go home, Dad was himself again.

"If you hadn't been punished enough already," he roared, "I'd give you a beating you'd never forget. What right did you have to play football? I've told you and told you to stay away from that game."

"It was only touch football," I said.

"Sure. Sure. 'Only touch football.' Nothing to it! Risk your whole career for a lousy game of touch football! I ought to knock you right into the middle of next week."

"He's all right now," I whispered to Ed. "Go ahead home. And thanks a million."

The next Tuesday I went to church and made a novena to St. Joseph that my wrist would be all right again. I made one every Tuesday until it had healed. I talked the doctor into taking the cast off after two weeks. Then I spent the next week soaking it in hot water. I played the first two games of the basketball season with the wrist taped up. But the kids on the opposing teams knew I'd broken it, and they chopped at it every chance they got. Just before the third game started, I got an inspiration. I taped up the *left* wrist. It worked fine. With everyone whacking at the good wrist, the bad one healed nicely.

It was a good year. Mom came home just before Christmas — she had been in and out of Norwich several times in the intervening years — and Dad, all wrapped up in our best basketball season, was in a good mood most of the time. Leavenworth High went to New Haven for the Connecticut schoolboy basketball championship tournament in March, and my father was there for the final round. Halfway through the game, I dislocated my jaw. The trainer came out and snapped it back into place on the spot. The sight was too much for Dad. He collapsed at his seat and had to be taken to the hospital. He had suffered a heart attack. I knew nothing about it until the game was over.

My dad's condition did not seem serious, and, at his insistence, I went to Boston the following week for the New England school basketball championship tournament. After winning the Connecticut title, we ripped through the Boston games, winning the finals when I scored twenty-nine points, seven in the last minute of play. We beat Durfee High School of Fall River, Massachusetts, 51–44. Those last seven points of mine gave us the title. The next morning the Boston papers hailed me as the hero of the tournament, and Boston fans saw my name in sports-page headlines for the first time.

But I wasn't happy. All I could think of was Mom and Dad and how much they needed me. We hadn't said anything, but college was out of the question. I'd have to make some quick money, and I'd have to keep on making it. I didn't know how long before Mom might have to go back to the hospital and Dad wouldn't be able to work any more. Only one thing pleased me. My mother was more like her old self than she had been in ten years. She seemed happy and calm as she worked around the house, and all of the old apprehension appeared to be gone.

Before my father came home from the hospital, I said to her, "I'm not going to college, Mom."

"Why?" she asked.

"I'll have to work."

"That's up to you, Jimmy. But go if you want to. We'll get along."

After my father got home I brought the subject up again.

"Do you *want* to go to college?" Dad asked.

"How can I go? There's no money in the bank."

"Well, it's for you to decide."

"I don't want to go to college, anyhow," I said, deliberately keeping my voice steady. "I don't like to study that much."

None of us ever mentioned it again.

During those last few weeks before I graduated from high school, I was more restless than ever. Night after night I tossed around for hours as I tried to figure out how I could play ball and still make enough money to support my folks. I didn't stop at trying to solve the problem of meeting current expenses. My head kept spinning with long-range worries about the family's permanent security. *How much would Dad and Mom need if they both were well? How much if Dad could never work again? How much if Mom had to go back to the hospital? How much to see that they always had a car? How much to get them out of that heatless, cold-water flat? How much could I collect for signing a baseball contract? How much did I want to collect? Would it ruin my career if I were a bonus player? If I weren't I'd have to get another job. And what kind of a job could I hope to get if I intended to tie myself up playing baseball seven months of the year? I needed money — plenty of money. How else could I set up my parents for life?*

The dollar signs weren't just dancing back and forth in the half-world between wakefulness and sleep which ruined my nights. They were being waved in my face during the days, too. After graduation the baseball

[47]

scouts closed in. Some talked big bonuses, but I was much too young for that. In those days, a bonus player — a boy who got more than six thousand dollars for signing a contract — couldn't play minor-league ball for more than one year. Then he had to go right to the major-league club that signed him. That would mean I'd be in the big leagues at eighteen, when I should be getting experience in the minors. I wouldn't be good enough to make a major-league club at that age. I would still be three or four years away. *What could I learn sitting on the bench, even a big-league bench? I couldn't accept a bonus. But if I didn't, what would I do for money?*

My problem was complicated by the fact that my dad thought I was too young to sign with anybody. On the day I graduated, he said, "Get a job this summer. You can play ball next year."

"How can I play ball next year if I lay off this year?" I demanded.

"Can't you get a job where you can work and play ball, too?"

"Where?"

"How do I know where? Look around. Maybe Tracy can help you."

But the next day I had to go to Boston to work out with the Braves. Billy Southworth, then the manager, wanted to see me. I spent a couple of hours at Braves Field, while he watched me make circus catches in the outfield and then gun the ball in. I hit the ball pretty well in batting practice, too. Southworth pulled me aside and asked, "How old are you, Jimmy?"

"Seventeen," I said.

"All right. We'll give you twenty thousand dollars to sign with us. Talk to your father when you get home, and let me know tomorrow."

Twenty thousand dollars! Wait'll Dad heard about this! We'd be on Easy Street.

But my dad was not impressed.

"To begin with," he pointed out, "you'd be a bonus player. After a year you'd rot on the Braves bench. In the second place, I want you to play with the Red Sox, not the Braves. And in the third place, you're still too young for professional baseball. I want you to work and play semi-pro baseball on the side this summer."

Within the next week, I got offers from the Detroit Tigers, the New York Yankees and the Brooklyn Dodgers. The Tigers and Yankee scouts mentioned bonuses, but named no figures. The Dodgers offered me a two-thousand-dollar advance against a three-year bonus contract at four thousand dollars a year, which would not have made me a bonus player. We didn't want to do anything until we heard from the Red Sox.

The Red Sox scout was a thin, slight man in his late thirties named Neil Mahoney. Both Dad and I had met him, and we both liked him immensely. He had jet-black hair, black eyebrows, sharp intense eyes and a sort of bittersweet smile. He talked in an even, low voice and, unlike the other scouts, he made no attempt to put any pressure on us.

He came in one day and started discussing the Red Sox.

"We've got a fine organization," he pointed out. "Our farm system is one of the best in baseball. You'll learn a lot on your way up, Jimmy."

"How long would it take him to reach the big leagues?" Dad asked.

"Usually about four years, depending on the boy. Of course, you can't foresee anything in this business, but if everything goes all right, it shouldn't take Jimmy any longer. And by the time he reaches the Red Sox, they'll be looking for outfielders. We've got two of the best in the world, Ted Williams and Dominic DiMaggio, but they're not going to last forever."

"Williams, DiMaggio — and Piersall," I said, slowly. "Holy cow! What an outfield!"

"I've heard worse," Mahoney nodded.

"We've had some pretty good offers," my father said. "What will the Red Sox do for us?"

"Three years at four thousand dollars a year. We'll give you two thousand dollars of it when you sign."

It was the identical terms the Dodgers had offered. I wanted to accept on the spot. But Dad said, "Jimmy isn't going to sign with anyone now."

"All right," said Neil, standing up to go. "But when he's ready, will you let me know?"

My father agreed. After Mahoney left, I said, "What do we do now?"

"I talked to Bill Tracy yesterday, and he can get a job for you. Go and see him."

Bill's brother Frank was assistant general manager of Factory H at the International Silver Company plant in nearby Meriden. He had an ideal job lined up for me. I would load freight cars during working hours and play ball for the company team, the Insilcos, several nights a week, for which I'd get extra money. On top of that there were other independent semi-pro teams around, and I could play for one of them when it didn't conflict with Insilco games.

We called Neil Mahoney and he came back to see us. My dad told him about the job. "Will the Red Sox let Jim sign a contract now, but not go into the organization until next spring?" he asked. "In that way, he could take this job now."

"That can be arranged all right," Mahoney agreed.

"And what about my dad?" I said, on an impulse. "I'd like to have him get a physical checkup."

"Tell you what we'll do," Neil said. "We'll send your father to the Lahey Clinic in Boston for a thorough checkup and pay all the bills. How would that be?"

That was the clincher. I signed with the Red Sox.

I went to work at Meriden a few days later, and I think it was then that I first really understood how utterly dependent on me my parents were. They were both incapacitated — my dad would never recover completely and I had no way of knowing how long Mom would continue to be all right — and the pressure was all on me to keep them going. Now I was assailed with new worries. *Suppose something should happen to me? Suppose I got sick? Suppose I got hurt and couldn't work or play ball? My folks needed me. I had to make all the money I could while I was still healthy. I couldn't waste a minute.*

I moved into higher gear than ever, rolling along at a mad pace, as I tore from one thing to another. I did everything on the run, yet lived such a tight schedule that I left myself only a few hours a night for sleeping. I'll never know how much actual sleep I got. I spent a lot of time lying down, but I was tense and stiff even then. I tried desperately to unwind. My nerves, stretched like fiddlestrings, were constantly begging for release.

My day started at five-thirty A.M. I had to be at the plant by seven. I worked there until five in the afternoon, then practiced for an hour or so. The Insilcos usually played three nights a week and I played for independent teams on the other nights. Every Sunday, I went to Hartford for a doubleheader with one club, and sometimes I'd play a third game with another team Sunday nights.

By going at top speed all the time, I could make as much as one hundred fifty dollars a week, but, as the summer progressed, I began to be plagued by new fears. *What would I do when the baseball season was over?* All I'd have then was my pay as a loader at the plant. *What would I do with the rest of my time? Whatever I did, I couldn't hope to make one hundred fifty dollars a week or anywhere near it.*

By this time, everyone who was close to me — Dad, Mom, Sister Margaret, the Tracys, Bernie — was trying to slow me down. No one — not even Sister Margaret — could do anything with me. I agreed that I was going too fast. I agreed that I was running around in a mad circle, using up every reserve of strength God had given me. I agreed that there was no point in trying to make more money if it meant a breakdown in my health. I agreed that there really was no urgency — I had set aside enough to get us through the winter — and even if I didn't work we'd be all right for a while. But I had to keep hurrying — hurrying nowhere — because I felt that if I didn't hurry, I couldn't keep alive. *I had to get things done.* It didn't matter what everyone said, or how much sense it made. With me, *everything* was urgent.

One day, my father warned, "If you don't slow down, you'll be dead tired when it comes time for spring training."

Spring training! The magic phrase made my spine tingle. I felt warm all over just thinking about it. *Spring training would be the real beginning of my career. That was what I'd always been aiming for. And in four years — the Red Sox outfield. Williams, DiMaggio — and Piersall!* I spoke the three names aloud. My dad smiled, and said, quietly, "You've got to take it easy, son."

I didn't exactly take it easy, but I managed to rein myself in a little. My job at the plant kept me busy days, and I made extra money and kept in good physical condition by refereeing basketball games a few nights a week. I still had the urge to move fast and crowd in as much as I could, but the thought of spring training and what it meant kept me from the dreadful compulsion that had transformed the summer into a nightmare. My nerves showed signs of loosening up a little and I slept better. Even the headaches were less severe, although they didn't disappear altogether. Best of all, Mom, rather than showing signs of a relapse, was becoming more and more of an influence in the household. She had new responsibilities now, and she seemed to thrive on them. I had no way of knowing it then, but her illness was virtually over. She never returned to the hospital. My father's heart attack had given her something to live for, since she had to take care of him. My mom has been mentally sound to this day.

As the time for spring training approached, I began getting jumpy again. I still had that fear of the unknown, the same fear that had engulfed me as I moved up from grade to grade through elementary school — the fear of making a big change. I was facing the most radical change of my life. I was to report to the Red Sox Louisville farm club, which was training at Bradenton, Florida. I had never been in the South. I had never seen a baseball training camp.

Suppose I didn't make the grade? What if I had to come home a failure? How could I face my dad and mom and my friends? What would I do if I couldn't play ball — spend the rest of my life loading freight cars? And how should I act in Bradenton? How should I dress? How should I react to the other guys? How could I tell which should be my friends and which should not? What should I say to newspapermen? Should I call the coaches by their first names or should I call them "Mister"? And what should I do if they overlooked me?

If they did overlook me, how could I attract attention? That was more important than anything. There'll be dozens of rookies at the training camp. Some must be at least as good as I. What if most were better? The best

[54]

boys got jobs on the best clubs. What if I ended up way down in the sticks somewhere, with some Class C or D club? What if I couldn't even qualify for that?

But, scared as I was, I couldn't wait to get to Florida. I was in such a hurry that I left a day ahead of time. The Red Sox had sent me my train ticket, Mom packed enough food to keep me going all the way down, and I took a ten-dollar bill with me. I didn't know that the ball club paid all the expenses. I thought just my transportation and hotel bill would be taken care of. The ten-dollar bill was for food. I didn't worry too much about what I'd do after I'd eaten it up. I figured that, if I had to, I could pick up an odd job here and there, and that would get me through the spring-training period.

Most of my stuff was in a steel foot locker, which I had shipped ahead. All I had with me on the train was the food and an overnight bag. I figured I'd pick up the foot locker at the Bradenton station after I arrived there.

The ten-dollar bill was still intact when I got off the train, but I didn't dare spend any of it on such a luxury as a taxi. The ball club was staying at the Dixie Grande Hotel, which wasn't far from the station, so I walked over to it. I was worried about the foot locker, though. The freight station at Bradenton was some distance from the passenger station, and about four miles from the hotel. At the Dixie Grande, the clerk, who told me that I was a day early and that none of the ballplayers were around, assigned me to my room, and, after leaving my overnight bag there, I went to get the foot locker.

It was a forty-minute walk to the freight station. I picked up the locker, hoisted it on my shoulders and started lugging it back to the Dixie Grande. The farther I walked the heavier it got and the slower I moved. I finally broke down and hailed a cab. The fare was thirty cents, and I had to go into the hotel to get my ten-dollar bill changed because the driver couldn't break it. Feeling like a maharajah, I gave him a nickel tip, and the cab driver rewarded me with a look nasty enough to make my hair curl. It didn't bother me any. I needed the money worse than he did.

I slept badly and woke up tired, taut and tense. After breakfast at a dog cart nearby, I went back to my room, wondering what to do next. While I was trying to make up my mind, my roommate walked in. He was a clean-cut looking guy, dressed as if he had a date with Miss Florida. His gray suit was neatly pressed, his two-toned shoes were spotlessly clean and he wore a white shirt with a necktie. He didn't seem to be much younger than Bill Tracy.

He held out his hand and said, "Chapman. Kenny Chapman. Call me Chappie."

"My name's Jimmy Piersall."

"Rookie."

He wasn't asking — just stating a fact.

"Uh-huh."

"I used to be one," he said.

"When?"

"About a million years ago."

While he was talking, he opened his suitcase and began to unpack. My eyes almost popped.

"What do you do with all those clothes?" I asked.

"Wear 'em," he said, laconically.

"Holy cow! Look at the creased trousers! How many pairs have you got?"

"Six or seven."

"What do you need all those for?"

He stopped unpacking for a minute, straightened up and asked, softly, "How old are you, Jimmy?"

"Eighteen."

"Where you from?"

"Waterbury, Connecticut."

"Ever been South with a ball club before?"

"No."

"How many pairs of — uh — creased trousers have you got?"

"One. And I don't wear those except for best."

He turned his head slowly from side to side, then grinned and said, "You've got a lot to learn, boy. I'm going to have to teach you some of the facts of life."

Before the day was over, I learned that the club paid for meals and laundry, and gave each player ten dollars a week for incidental expenses. There were no rules about dressing, but you were supposed to look neat and act like a gentleman. The Louisville Colonels were in the American Association, a Triple A league. At the time, it was the highest you could get in baseball without being in the major league.

I also learned that it was practically a certainty that I wouldn't be assigned to the Louisville club.

"The Red Sox own teams in leagues of every classification," Chappie told me. "They'll look you over here, and then probably send you to Coco, where their other clubs train."

"Where's Coco?"

"Not far from here. Other side of the state."

"How low can you get?" I asked.

"Don't worry," he said, kindly. "If you show them anything, they won't send you too far down. You're pretty young, Jimmy."

Rooming with Chappie was the best thing that could have happened to me. He had spent most of his years in the Red Sox organization as the Louisville third baseman, since he was never quite good enough for the big leagues. But he knew his way around, and he was generous with his advice and encouragement.

"Don't sell yourself short, Jimmy," he said, after he had seen me work out a few times. "You're a lot better than you think you are. You're not a bad hitter and you're the best fielder on the whole squad. All you need is experience and confidence in yourself. Don't forget, those other rookies are just as scared as you — and none of them can hold your glove."

On my first time at bat in the first intra-squad game, I hit a triple over the center fielder's head, and from then on I was all right. I was still tense and scared, but I had better control of my nerves and my headaches weren't too bad.

[58]

At the end of three weeks, I was sent to Coco and assigned to the Scranton club in the Class A Eastern League. I was satisfied, for it meant that I had made a better impression on the coaches than the other rookies. Practically all of them were sent to teams in leagues of lower classification.

The Scranton manager was Mike Ryba, one of the kindest, most considerate men I have ever known. Mike's homely face was nearly always wreathed in a wide-mouthed grin. He had a string of gold teeth, which he flashed often. His weatherbeaten face was deeply tanned from many years in the sun, and his almost coal-black eyes were set in a wreath of crow's feet, mementos of many years of smiling. As a boy, Mike had worked in the Pennsylvania anthracite mines, and baseball, to him, was more than just a profession. It was a way of life, and he never stopped talking about how wonderful it was.

"You're a lucky guy if you can play ball well enough to make a living out of it," he used to say. "And if you're good enough to get into the big leagues, where you eat and sleep and travel and live like a millionaire and get treated like the pampered son of a millionaire wherever you go, you ought to get down on your knees every day of your life and thank your God because He made you that way."

Mike had closed his active major-league career as a pitcher with the Red Sox, and previous to that, he had been a baseball jack-of-all-trades. He once played a different position in each inning of a full nine-inning game. He's the manager of the Houston club in the Texas League now, and I still run into him from time to time. Whenever I ask him how he is, he answers, "O.K. Why shouldn't I be? I'm eatin' regular and livin' good. You always do in this business."

A simple man who appreciates the simple things in life, I guess Mike is still baseball's champion hotel-lobby sitter. Except when he goes to and from the ball park or the railroad station or airport, Mike spends practically all his time in a lobby chair, calmly pulling away at a big black cigar. I asked him once if he didn't ever get curious about what goes on elsewhere in town.

"Why should I?" he answered. "I can see all I want to see from the lobby. One time in Boston I saw thirty-nine June weddings without moving out of my seat. Where else but in a lobby can you watch thirty-nine weddings in one month?"

Mike took an interest in me, partly because he thought I was a good ballplayer on the way up, partly because he realized how desperately I needed help and encouragement, and partly because I was his kind of guy. I used to lay all my problems in his lap while he sat, solid and serene, listening to my troubles and smoking his big black cigar. He would let me talk myself out. When I got all through, he'd roll the cigar around in his hand, take a couple of slow drags, let the smoke drift out of his mouth and finally drawl in his low, gravelly voice, "Nothing ever goes so wrong that it won't get right somehow. If you can't make it right, wait a little while and it'll right itself." Mike couldn't solve all my problems, but he was good for my nerves. Just looking at him relieved some of the tensions that were always tying me up inside.

When we first went to Scranton, I moved into a rooming house with Nylon Smith, a left-handed pitcher about my age. We stayed together only about a week, because Smitty was sent down to another club, but it turned out to be the most important week of my life. It was during that week that I met the remarkable girl who later became my wife.

Except for Sundays, the Scranton club played all-night games, and after we showered and dressed, we used to go to a restaurant called the Tiptoe for a bite to eat and a chance to relax. I was standing outside the place waiting for Smitty one night, when a neat-looking guy who walked with a limp came over to me, held out his hand and asked, "Aren't you Jimmy Piersall?"

"That's right."

"My name's Tony Howley. I go to all the Red Sox games."

He meant the Scranton Red Sox, who were named after the parent club in Boston.

We talked until Smitty came along, and then Tony went into the Tiptoe with us. I told him I wanted to go to confession, and he arranged to meet me the next day so he could take me to St. Anne's Monastery. It turned out that Tony, who was an accountant, had once studied to be a priest, but he had lost a leg in an accident, so he had to give it up.

Smitty and I walked into the Tiptoe a couple of nights later, and Tony was sitting at his big table with a group

[61]

of girls and boys. He waved to us, then came over to say hello. After a while he said, "I'll see you guys later. I've got to go back to my date."

"Which one's your date?" I asked.

"The little one over in the corner."

"You mean the redhead?"

"I guess she's sort of redheaded, at that," Tony remarked. "Funny — I've known her for years and never noticed. Well — I'll see you."

I wanted to follow him and meet the redhead, but I didn't dare. I hadn't had much experience with girls. The only one I'd ever gone out with much was a Waterbury schoolmate named Pat Delaney. She and I grew up together. Our folks were friends, and I guess they hoped maybe we'd get married some day. We liked each other all right, but if I ever had the remotest idea of getting serious with her, I forgot all about it one night during my senior year in high school.

"What are you going to do after you graduate?" she asked.

"Gee, I don't know. Play ball, I suppose."

"Ballplayers are traveling all the time, aren't they?"

"Yes."

"I wouldn't want to marry a ballplayer. Ballplayers aren't home enough."

"Well," I said, "I'm going to be a ballplayer."

And that was that.

Every so often I stole looks at the little redhead with Tony. Her hair was really light brown, I suppose, but it had a reddish cast to it. She had huge china-blue eyes, shining white teeth, high cheekbones, and soft white skin. I thought she was the most beautiful girl I'd ever seen, but all I could do that night was sit and admire her from a distance.

"Nice, huh?"

Smitty was pointing towards her. I reddened and clenched my fists but I didn't say anything. *I'm mad at Smitty and I don't even know the girl. And all he said was what I was thinking.*

At the Tiptoe the next night, I said to Tony, "That your girl — the one you were with last night?"

"Heck, no," he replied. "I don't have any girl. She's just an old friend."

"Who is she, what does she do, and when are you going to introduce us?"

"Her name's Mary Teevan. She's training to be a nurse. You like her, eh? She's a nice girl. I'll take her to the ball game and introduce you to her later if you'll promise to hit a home run tomorrow night."

"I'll promise anything."

The next night I hit a home run my first time up. When Smitty and I walked into the Tiptoe after the game, Tony beckoned to us. His cousin Bob Howley, who drove us home every night, was with him, along with Mary and a couple I'd seen before but had never met. The girl's name was Ann O'Brien and the boy with her was Dan Kuchar. I didn't pay much attention to either of them. I was too busy edging Tony away from the chair beside Mary. He caught on quickly and made room for me. I sat down, tried to think of something sensationally clever

[63]

to say, grinned foolishly at Mary, took a deep breath and finally managed a brilliantly conceived, "Holy cow!"

Mary laughed.

"I liked your home run," she said. It was the first time I'd ever heard her speak. Her voice sounded just the way I expected — neat and small and calm, yet clear and direct.

"So did I," I replied. Then I said, "I wouldn't have hit it except I wanted to meet you."

"Tony told me. He knows lots of girls. Get him to introduce you to one a day. It'll make you the greatest home-run hitter of all time."

A day or so later, I was walking along Washington Street, the main thoroughfare in Scranton, when I heard a girl say, "Holy cow! Look who's here."

It was Mary, smiling as she used my favorite expression. She was on her way to the hospital with Ann, who was also in training to be a nurse. I persuaded them to stop in at a soda fountain, but they were in a hurry and only had time for a Coke. While they were drinking, I gobbled up two sundaes and was just starting on an ice-cream soda when they got up to leave. The last thing Mary said as she walked out was, "Holy cow! What an appetite!"

I may not have liked the way he said it, but Smitty was right. This is a nice girl. This is more than that. This is the girl for me. Mary Teevan. Catholic — like me. That's good. I'm going to marry a Catholic. Marry? How can I think of marriage? I've got enough other re-

sponsibilities without taking on any more. I have to take care of Mom and Dad. But I wonder. Maybe I can't think of marriage now. But I want to know more about Mary Teevan. What does she like? What doesn't she like? Where is she from? How about her people? When can I see her again? I've got to call her up and make a date — for tonight. She'll be through at the hospital at just about the same time the ball game's over. But where does she live? I don't even know the name of her hospital.

I called Tony Howley, and he said I could reach Mary at St. Mary's Hospital, so I phoned her just before I left to go to the ball park that night. As I waited for her to come to the phone I nearly hung up. My hand was shaking so much that I couldn't get a firm grip on the receiver, and suddenly I seemed to be swimming in perspiration. When she finally answered in her small, firm voice, I could only stammer, "Meet me at the Tiptoe after work?"

"Holy cow!" she said. "It's Jimmy again. How are you?"

"O.K. Meet me, Mary?"

"Sure. I'll meet you, Jimmy," she said, softly.

"And if the game's not over —"

"I don't have to go back on duty until tomorrow afternoon, so I don't care how late I get in. If the game's not over, Jimmy, I'll wait for you."

There was a caress in her voice, and somehow I didn't feel nervous any more. I wanted to stand in that phone booth and talk to her, but I had to get to the ball park.

[65]

"Mary —" I said.

"What?"

"Uh — nothing. I'll see you at the Tiptoe."

My heart was pounding when I hung up. *What's the matter with me? I never felt this way about a girl before.*

At the Tiptoe, Mary was sitting at a table in the corner, with Ann and Tony and Dan and a couple of other people. She waved when I walked in, and motioned me to an empty chair beside her. I was annoyed. I'd hoped to find her alone. I nodded to everyone else, and greeted Mary with a somewhat thin "Hi." Then I sat down.

The conversation was general, but I didn't have much to say, even though everyone was talking about the ball game. I couldn't take my eyes off Mary. I saw now that her hair wasn't really red at all, but quite definitely brown. I loved to watch her smile, for she smiled with more than just her mouth. Her eyes twinkled and her whole face lit up, and she smiled often. For the first time, I noticed the curve of her chin. She had a look of determination, and I saw now that it was because of her chin. It was a beautiful chin and it went well with the rest of her face because it didn't jut out, but it just missed being square. *I wonder if she's stubborn. Does she have to have her own way all the time?* She smiled and I relaxed. *How can a girl with a smile like that be stubborn?*

"Are you always so happy?" I asked.

"Are you always so serious?" she countered.

We both laughed. Then I said, "Let's go somewhere and talk."

"Can't we talk here?"

"Not really," I said. "All these people —"

"We can't very well break away."

"Why not?"

"Wouldn't it be sort of obvious?"

"What if it is?"

"Jimmy —"

"What?"

"After tomorrow, I go back on duty days."

"Then we can get together Sunday night. There's no ball game."

"Holy cow, you're a real bright boy, aren't you?"

We both laughed again. It wasn't until after Bob Howley had driven her home and then dropped me off at my rooming house that I realized my tensions and pressures had eased up so much that I was almost completely relaxed.

At the time, Mary was living with an aunt, Mary Holleran. We sat on the porch Sunday evening, and talked softly while a full moon played hide-and-seek with passing clouds. One minute it would be almost pitch dark and the next the whole porch would be glowing. I remember that evening very well because it was the first time I ever talked frankly about myself to a girl my own age; in fact, before I was through, I told Mary things I had never told another living soul. I told her about my headaches and my fears and my mom's trouble and my dad's temper and my need for security and my everlasting quest for release from the pressures that plagued me. I tried to tell her everything at once. I was terribly anxious for her to know and understand me — the sooner the better.

[67]

Suddenly, I realized what I was doing and stopped, embarrassed because I had poured my troubles into her lap.

"I'm sorry," I said.

"Why?"

"I've talked all about myself. I must have been boring you."

"You haven't bored me, Jimmy. I want to know more."

"What about you? I don't know anything about you — except that you're in training to be a nurse. Tell me about yourself now."

"There isn't very much —"

She told me about her dad in Wilkes-Barre, and her younger brother Harry and still younger sister Ann. Her mother had died when she was eleven, and from then on there had always been a housekeeper. Her father had a good job. He was a dragline operator at a surface mine. A dragline, she explained, was a sort of super-steam shovel which was used to scoop up piles of coal residue. It took a skilled man to operate one — a man with keen long-distance eyesight and quick reactions.

"My dad's a little man, but he runs one of the biggest machines at the mines," she said. "And you know what, Jimmy? He's a great baseball fan. He goes to all the Wilkes-Barre games he can. He's seen you play."

"I can't have your dad rooting for Wilkes-Barre."

"He won't be. He's coming here to live in a few weeks — as soon as the kids get out of school."

I liked Mary's father. As she had explained, he was a small man, but he didn't seem small, for he carried himself with dignity. He had merry eyes which glinted with good humor, and a leisurely manner of talking which gave the impression that he never was in a hurry to finish a sentence. It was easy to see where Mary had acquired her smile. Her dad's eyes never stopped smiling, and his mobile face relaxed often into a wide grin. His real name was Harry, but for no particular reason, I started calling him George. Mary and I both call him George to this day.

I went with Mary all summer. Realizing my hunger for peace of mind, she was always trying to quiet me down and softly telling me to take it easy. She knew I was moving too fast, and time and again she said, "It's a long life, Jimmy. Don't try to use it up all at once."

We grew closer and closer, and I was happy in the knowledge that I had found the girl I wanted. Mary was my kind of person — a member of my faith, a child of a working-class family and a product of a medium-sized city. We understood each other so well that we drifted into talk of marriage as naturally as we talked of everything else.

One night I said, "We could be happy together."

"Could we?"

"Yes. Only —"

"Only what, Jimmy?"

"Well — I don't have very much money. And I've got to take care of my folks."

"I know."

"We might even have to live with them."

"That's all right."

"Someday, Mary — not this year, but maybe next — all right?"

I went back to work for the silver company in Meriden during the winter of 1948–1949, and, to make sure that Mary wouldn't forget me, I bought a second-hand car and commuted between Waterbury and Scranton every other weekend. It was a tough, eight-hour trip over winding, mountainous roads. I would drive to Scranton Saturday, stay there until Sunday evening and then go directly to Meriden, walking into the plant on Monday morning without any sleep. It was not recommended routine for a boy suffering from nervous tension, but, even though I was usually too tired to take Mary anywhere after arriving in Scranton, I thrived on it. I was more relaxed that winter than I had been for years.

I was apprehensive about my father's reaction to Mary, so I didn't tell him how serious I felt about her. But between his illness and my own new-found independence, he no longer could frighten me with his roaring temper. He told me what he thought I should do, and if I thought his advice was good, I followed it.

When it came time for spring training, I reported back to the Louisville club. I was looking forward to it because Mike Ryba had been made manager of the Colonels. To make me feel even more at home, Ed Doherty, who was president of the Scranton club when I played there, had also been promoted to Louisville. Doherty, a tall, friendly, prematurely gray man who always treated me well, is now president of the American Association.

A month after the 1949 season started, Mary flew to Louisville to see me. She stayed with friends for several days, and just before she flew back I said, "How about setting a date?"

"Like right after the season's over?"

"Yes — sometime in October."

The next time she came to Louisville, my dad was there. He had met Mary in Scranton, and was not upset when I told him we were going to get married. It wouldn't have made any difference, of course, but I was relieved because I had been apprehensive about his reaction. I knew there'd be no trouble with Mom. She and Mary got along very well, and, in fact, Mom already was aware of our plans and approved of them.

I was very happy, even though assailed by vague worries over finances. I was assuming a new responsibility, but Mary was so willing to co-operate that I almost felt that I was taking advantage of her. Each time I started to tell her about my obligations in Waterbury, she put a finger to my lips and said, "Don't worry about it, honey. Whatever you say is all right with me. Don't you know that yet?"

I did know it, but I still couldn't help worrying about money. Occasionally, while I tossed around trying to get to sleep at night, I'd be plagued by simple mathematics, as I tried to figure out how much I'd have to give the folks, how much we'd need to live on, how much I could put into the bank and how much more I could make over my baseball salary.

One day I asked my father, "How much do you need every week? Tell me exactly."

"Thirty-five dollars," he replied.

"O.K."

After that I did all my nocturnal figuring with that as a base. *After I had set aside thirty-five dollars for my parents, how much would Mary and I need to live on? And how long would there just be the two of us? We both wanted a family. How much more would it cost to have one? And what if one of us should get sick? How could I possibly figure out how much that would set us back? No matter what happened, the thirty-five dollars for Mom and Dad would have to be taken out. That was a prime responsibility.*

But whenever I brought up the subject of money with Mary, she laughed it off.

"Don't lose any sleep over it," she insisted. "We'll get along."

"I know, but I want you to have a nice place to live. Honey, I've got to make a lot of money."

"You will. I know you will."

"We'll have to live with Mom and Dad, and I hate to think of your being in that flat."

She kept assuring me that it was all right, but the more I thought about it the less I liked the idea. Mary would never be happy on East Main Street, no matter what she said to the contrary. I began to wonder if I could swing a house. I had some cash in the bank and if I could work out reasonable payments —

WE WERE married on October 22 at the Church of the Nativity of Our Lord in Scranton. Mary's cousin Ruth Holleran was maid of honor, and Tony Howley was my best man. The priest who married us was the Reverend John O'Brien, Ann's brother. Father O'Brien had become a good friend of mine. He later officiated when his sister married Dan Kuchar.

A number of people came over from Waterbury. My folks, and one of my aunts — my mother's sister — were there, and so was Bernie Sherwill. Al Dostaler, who had played on the Leavenworth High School basketball team with Bernie and me, the Tracys, and Jarp O'Neil came, too, along with several family friends. It was a wonderful wedding and everyone, including me, was very happy.

Back in Waterbury, we moved in with my parents, and I went back to my old job at the plant in Meriden. I kept thinking about the possibility of buying a new house, but I knew I couldn't afford it yet, so I didn't say anything to Mary. Then, right after Christmas, Mary told me there was a baby on the way. For three weeks, I walked around on air, but my happiness didn't last any longer than that. Mary got sick a month before it was time to go South to start training for the 1950 season, and for a while her condition was pretty serious. I spent my days at the hospital and my nights alternately praying and ripping my jagged nerve ends apart with frantic worry. She lost the baby, of course, but by that time I just wanted her to get well. She

[73]

improved enough to go to spring training with me, but she wasn't herself, since she tired easily and still had a lot of pain. The Colonels were training at Deland, Florida, that year, and the doctors thought it would do Mary good to be where the weather was mild.

Mary's recovery was slow — much too slow. She still wasn't right when we got to Louisville for the opening of the season, and she was so shaky that I dreaded every trip we had to make. Then in May she got sick again, and this time the situation was desperate. For days she lived on other people's blood, as she had to have one transfusion after another. Her life hung in the balance and so did my sanity. I couldn't concentrate on anything, even baseball. All I could do was go to the hospital, stare at Mary, head for the ball park when it was time for the game, go through the motions of playing and then go through the motions of trying to sleep. I dreaded the proximity of a telephone for fear that someone would reach me with bad news.

After a few days, I began to develop stomach pains myself. I didn't dare tell Ryba about them, because I was afraid he would bench me, but I couldn't fool Mike for long. He knew Mary was very sick, and all he had to do was look at me to realize that I was pretty badly off myself.

"Go home," he said one night. "Don't come back until Mary's out of danger."

"But my job —" I started to object.

"Forget your job. It'll be here when you get back."

The next few days seemed like months, and I couldn't

begin to estimate how much they took out of me. All I know is that life had turned into an everlasting vigil of prayer, desperate hope and nerve-racking worry while my head pounded with pressure and my stomach writhed with pain. Then, one morning, good news came. A nurse met me on Mary's floor and whispered, "She's going to be all right."

For the first time in a week, I smiled. I stayed with Mary most of the day, and then, my stomach pains gone, I had my first square meal since she had taken sick. That night I told Mike I was ready, and he put me back in center field. At Mary's insistence and with the doctor's approval I made the next road trip. By the time I returned to Louisville, she was fine. She had made a miraculous, almost unbelievable recovery.

The Red Sox, who were on the road, sent for me early in September, and I joined them in Chicago. While I was thrilled over the prospect of traveling in the same company with men like Williams and DiMaggio, I suffered from nothing worse than the usual jitters that always engulfed me before making a major change. Big-league ball clubs often bring youngsters up from their farm teams in September so that managers can see them work out after they have been playing the better part of a full season in the minors. My being included in the 1950 crop was not unexpected, since, in spite of my personal troubles, I had had a good year under Ryba in Louisville.

The Red Sox manager was Steve O'Neill, a battered old baseball warhorse who had been in the majors as player, coach and manager for more than forty years. A former catcher, his nose was squashed and twisted and every one of his fingers gnarled and bent from frequent bone breaks. Like Ryba, he was a product of the Pennsylvania coal-mine regions. He had been around the majors for so long that he had become a sort of baseball nomad, never in or out of a job for any length of time. The Red Sox were the third team he managed and he has since been in and out of Philadelphia, where he managed the Phillies for a couple of seasons.

Steve, the patriarch of a huge family, liked rookies and knew how to handle them. A jovial, good-humored man, he rarely got annoyed and I never saw him lose his temper. He was always considerate and kind to me.

"You won't get to play much, son," he told me, "but you'll learn a lot by sitting on the bench and keeping your eyes open. You'd be surprised how much you can pick up just by watching what goes on around you."

I was so happily simply wearing a Red Sox uniform that, for once, the prospect of sitting on the bench most of the time didn't bother me. The season had only a few weeks to go and, as Steve pointed out, I could learn by looking. Besides, he told me I might get a chance to pinch-hit a few times, and maybe even start in one of the late-season games.

But I didn't get my name into a big-league box score until the last week of the season. We were playing the Washington Senators in Boston, when, during the third inning of a hopelessly lost game, O'Neill sent me up to bat for our pitcher, Dick Littlefield. Gene Bearden, a veteran who threw a baffling knuckle ball, was the Washington pitcher, and I was so scared that I threw the bat over the third-base dugout and into the grandstand the first time I swung at a ball. Imagine my embarrassment when I found myself standing at the plate without a bat in my hand.

I turned and walked over to Billy Goodman, the next hitter. He had been crouching in the on-deck circle, but he stood up and met me halfway.

"What do I do now?" I whispered.

"Get another bat," said Billy. "Here — use mine."

I did, and it brought me luck. After the count ran to three balls and two strikes, I drove the ball safely to right field for a hit on my first time at bat in the majors. I felt as if I were flying down the first-base line — there were wings on my shoulders.

When I said good-by to O'Neill after the last game of the season, he shook hands and said, "You'll get there, boy. We'll see you next spring in Sarasota."

Mary and I went back to Waterbury again after the season was over, both of us bubbling with happy anticipation. We were expecting again, and this time the doctors assured us that everything would be all right. Furthermore, we had decided to buy a home. We found a new ranch-type house that was not quite completed. The builder assured us we could get in before Christmas, so we settled down with my folks while we waited. Mom and Dad were going to move in with us, and I was glad I could get them out of their old apartment.

Mary, busy with decorating and furnishing the new

place, was having a wonderful time. I went back to work for International Silver, so we had that additional income, and there was really no financial problem, but I had misgivings. Something seemed to be wrong somewhere, and I couldn't figure out what it was. I should have been happy. Mary was out of the woods and a baby was on the way. I was moving my parents out of an ancient flat where they had lived for years. I was about to go into a brand new home, complete with the latest gadgets and equipment. I was in my own home town, among my own people, and working at a familiar off-season job. Everything should have been perfect.

It wasn't. Night after night, after Mary was asleep, I would lie in bed, tossing around and worrying about the house. *Was I doing the right thing? Would I be able to meet the payments? Would Mary be happy once we were settled down? Did I want to commit myself to living in Waterbury permanently? A house was a pretty permanent thing. Once in there, would it be easy to get out? Yet why should I want to get out? How could I be thinking of getting out? I hadn't even moved in. What was the matter with me?*

All through the month of November, while Mary kept going back and forth between East Main Street and the new house, I worried about the situation. She was so happy getting ready to move in that I didn't have the heart to tell her about my doubts. Instead, I listened while she chattered, telling me about the furniture and the drapes and the colors and the kitchen equipment and all the other things wives talk about that go in one male ear and out the other.

The weeks went by quickly, and one day when I got home Mary met me with a breathless, "The house is ready. We can go in tomorrow."

"Tomorrow?"

I didn't expect it to happen so fast.

"Oh, there are a few little odds and ends, but we can take care of them after we move in. Oh, Jimmy, I'm so happy!"

"Well," I said. "That's fine." And, as if to convince myself, I said it again.

We didn't move in the next day, but the day after. It was December 15, and Mom and Dad were busy getting ready to leave their apartment, but they wouldn't be completely set for several days. However, they would be back and forth all the time, and it wouldn't take them long to get settled.

On the day we moved, I suddenly realized what had been bothering me. *I was trapped. We both were trapped — Mary and I — if we bought that house. If we bought it? What was I thinking? We had bought it already. And, for no one knew how many more years, I would have to listen to the rasping, nagging voice of my father hollering at my mom, telling her what she was doing wrong, just as he had been telling her what was wrong as long as I could remember. Suppose he started nagging Mary? I couldn't live with him any more. I loved him and I loved Mom, and I wanted them both to live a long time. But if I had to listen to them arguing any more, I'd be wishing they were dead so Mary and I could get out from under. Why, we'd be counting the years! What could I do? I couldn't tell them now they weren't to move in with us. There was only one answer. We'd have to sell the house.*

I told Mary the next day.

"Honey," I said, "we can't stay here."

"Can't stay here?" Her voice was shaking. "Honey, what do you mean? What's the matter?"

"We can't afford it," I said, a little too sharply.

"But I thought we could afford it. We had it all figured out. Between the baseball income and the winter job, we're in good shape. And you don't have to worry about giving your folks so much money every week, because they'll be living with us."

"It would be better for me to give them the thirty-five dollars a week."

"No, it wouldn't, Jimmy. We'll be happy here. It's just what we want."

"It isn't that," I said. "I simply can't afford to keep it, that's all."

"We can't afford not to keep it. We've spent a small fortune on household furnishings and things like that. We've made a big down payment. We've got a lot of money sunk in this house, honey."

"We can get it out. It's brand new. We won't have any trouble selling it. Mary —"

"What?"

"Let's get out of here. I want to get out of this house — out of this town — away from everything —"

"But Jimmy, I thought —"

"You were wrong. *Mary, we've got to sell the house. Do you understand?*"

Three days after we moved in, we moved out. We went to Scranton, and settled down with Mary's family. My mother and father returned to East Main Street. Several months later, we got our price and sold the house, furnishings and all.

Mary was puzzled and unhappy. She told me years later that she first began worrying about my health that day when I insisted on selling the house we had just bought. While she knew I was unusually tense and nervous, she had never seen me do anything so obviously irrational, and she was deeply concerned. But I was so much more at ease in Scranton than I had been in Waterbury that she stifled her original impulse, which had been to ask me to seek medical advice.

Anxious to be in the best possible physical condition, I started working out daily at the Catholic Youth Center gymnasium in Scranton. I had no illusions about making the Red Sox ball club that year. I was only twenty-one and had just two years of professional baseball behind me. But I wanted to make a good impression. As always when I was facing a change, I was apprehensive.

On top of that, I was worried about Mary again, for our first baby was expected in March. I had to report on March 1, but I was reluctant to leave her. But she and her father both insisted that I go, and when her doctor assured me that everything would be all right, I left for Florida. Four days after I arrived in Sarasota on March

5, 1951, I got the phone call I was waiting for. It was Mary herself. She told me that she had presented me with a daughter that morning. We called her Eileen.

With that burden off my mind, I concentrated on baseball. Payne Field, where the Red Sox train, has a huge expanse of outfield, and I had a wonderful time roaming all over it to catch fly balls. Lost in the sheer joy of grabbing them, I didn't realize what kind of impression I might be making on anyone who was watching me.

One day, after he had seen me in action for a week or so, Dominic DiMaggio, the Red Sox veteran center fielder and one of my baseball idols, came over to me and said, "Kid, from what I saw of you in Boston last year and here this spring, you're the best center fielder in the American League right now."

I thanked him and strutted off, glowing all over with pride. Talk about praise from Caesar! The man I most admired as a fielder, the man beside whom I had wanted to play almost as long as I could remember, had just paid me the supreme compliment. Dominic DiMaggio had, in effect, told me that I was even better than he was himself. What more could I ask?

As the time for cutting down the squad approached, I tensed up, expecting the ax to fall any day. But I was not in the first batch of men to go, nor was I in the second. Steve O'Neill didn't spend too much time with me but, judging by the fact that he kept me with the Red Sox, he apparently was satisfied.

One day he said, "You're a big-league fielder right now, Jimmy, but I want you to become a pull hitter. If you can learn to do that, you might make this club sooner than you expect."

I was a right-handed batter, but what is known in baseball terms as a "straightaway" hitter — in other words, I was inclined to swing late at the ball, and it would go either to center field or to the right of center. A right-handed "pull" hitter, on the other hand, could snap his bat around so fast that the ball would go to left field.

The Red Sox were always looking for right-handed batters who could pull the ball, for Fenway Park in Boston, their home park, has a short left-field fence. A good pull hitter could hit it often for extra bases and, if he had enough power, could clear it for home runs. If I could learn to pull the ball consistently, I'd become a valuable asset to the ball club.

O'Neill encouraged me, and when it came time to break camp at Sarasota I was still with the Red Sox. We barnstormed our way north, and I got into several exhibition games. We were scheduled to open the season in New York against the Yankees on April 17, two days after our last exhibition game, which was against the Braves in Boston. I hadn't seen Eileen yet, so O'Neill at my request gave me permission to go to Scranton after the last Braves game on the fifteenth. I was to meet the team in New York in time for the opener. That started me off on an intensive, nerve-racking week of mad driving which, to begin with, found me commuting between New York and Scranton, a little matter of four hours each way.

I drove to New York from Scranton the morning of the seventeenth, a Tuesday, and then went back home after the game. I did the same thing the next day. I got a break when it rained on Thursday. Although I had to drive to New York again, the game was postponed, so I got an early start back to Scranton. I needed it, since I had to be at Fenway Park in time for the Boston opening on Friday. I picked up Mary and Eileen, dumped our luggage into the car and drove through to Boston, getting in well after midnight on Thursday. I was dead tired when I got there. I had driven some six hundred miles without relief and I was so tense that I couldn't sleep even the few hours I allowed myself after we arrived in Boston.

In the meantime, it was obvious that I was going to have to spend a lot of time riding the Red Sox bench. Instead of Williams, DiMaggio and Piersall, the opening-day outfield consisted of Williams, DiMaggio and Billy Goodman. Four days after the season began, Goodman was shifted to first base, but Clyde Vollmer, a big right-handed power hitter, replaced Goodman in right field.

Two days after we got to Boston, I went to O'Neill and said, "When am I going to get into a ball game?"

"When I can find a spot for you," Steve replied.

"I know, but meanwhile I have to sit on the bench." I was nearly crying.

"Don't get discouraged, Jimmy," he said, kindly. "You're just a young fellow. You've got a lot to learn. I want you to sit and watch these fellows for a while."

"Steve, I can't stand sitting and watching other guys play ball. I've got to get in there myself. Please — if you don't intend to play me, send me somewhere else."

O'Neill looked sharply at me, then said, "You mean you want to go back to the minors?"

"I'd rather play there than sit and do nothing here."

He called me into his office after the ball game that day. "O.K., Jimmy," he said. "You're going to Louisville."

We left town that night. I wanted to drive straight through, but Mary made me stop on the way so I could get at least a few hours sleep. I reported back to the Colonels the next afternoon.

But the situation there had changed. Ryba had gone with the St. Louis Cardinals as a coach, and Mike Higgins was the new manager of the Louisville club. He is now manager of the Red Sox, and we get along very well. But in 1951, he wasn't too happy to see me. The Colonels had a big, right-handed batting pull hitter named Karl Olson, and Mike wanted to use him in center field. My appearance on the scene complicated matters since Higgins had to put me back in action.

Aside from the fact that I upset his plans, Mike didn't find me easy to take. I was a scared, tense kid who had just been through a series of shattering experiences. I made Higgins nervous with my perpetual moving around, my constant yelling, my everlasting restlessness and my eternal rush to get things done.

I knew the pressure was on me if I wanted to keep the center fielder's job. I had to hit the ball hard or be benched, and I was not a slugger. I fought a hopeless battle, knowing from the start that I couldn't win it. Sooner or later, I was bound to be replaced. As it was, I played in seventeen games at Louisville and batted .310, which is more than adequate in any league under normal circumstances, but Olson had to get his chance, and Higgins finally took me out. At the time I resented it, but, looking back on what happened, I realize that he had no alternative.

Now I was back on the bench, and it wasn't even the Red Sox bench. I was thoroughly confused, completely frustrated and very close to panic-stricken. A few days before we were to go on a road trip, I said to Mary, "I'm going to have to get out of here."

"Where can we go now?" she asked.

"I don't know. But it's got to be somewhere where I can play. I've got to get off the bench."

"What are you going to do?"

"Ask Ed Doherty to help me."

I talked to Doherty on the day before we left town, and our conversation was similar to the one I had had only a few weeks before with O'Neill.

"I can't afford to sit on the bench," I said. "I've got a wife and baby and parents to support. Will you send me out?"

"Well, I can't send you up, Jimmy," he replied. "It'll have to be down to a team in a league of lower classification than we are."

"As long as I play every day," I told him, "I don't care if it's Class D."

I was terribly depressed when we went on the road. On the train to Indianapolis, I sat by myself and stared out the window. I was mentally upset and physically uncomfortable, since I perspired so freely that I was soaking wet

[86]

half an hour after we left Louisville. *I've got four mouths to feed besides my own. How can I do it on a minor-league salary? And now I can't even make the best minor-league team in the Red Sox organization. I'm nowhere nearly ready for the majors — not if I'm not good enough for Louisville. I can't get anywhere from the Colonels bench. Where can I go from Louisville? As Doherty pointed out, it had to be down, not up. And how far down will I have to go?*

By the time we arrived in Indianapolis, I was so distraught that I phoned Mary and asked her to drive up with the baby. It was only one hundred miles. She promised to come the next day, and told me to expect her in the early afternoon. Before she arrived, I had orders to report to the Birmingham Barons in the Class Double A Southern Association, one grade below the Triple A American Association.

I was standing in front of the Hotel Lincoln in Indianapolis when Mary drove up at about two in the afternoon. Eileen was in the back seat, fast asleep. I opened the trunk of the car, swung my bag in, slid under the wheel and, after a quick greeting, stepped on the gas.

"Where are we going?" Mary asked.

"Back to Louisville."

"Then where?"

"Birmingham," I said.

The next thirty hours were a rolling nightmare. We became slaves to an automobile, eating little and sleeping less as we made the long haul to the Deep South. We spent most of the night packing in Louisville, since Mary had got settled in an apartment there only the week before. Then, after a couple of hours' sleep, we piled into the car and set sail for Birmingham.

I drove all the way, and I couldn't have told you the route we followed an hour after we arrived. Louisville to Birmingham is something over four hundred miles, and I was determined to get there in time for the game that night. Except for a few stops for gasoline and sandwiches, I drove steadily and without relief. Mary wanted to take the wheel, but I wouldn't let her. I was afraid she wouldn't go fast enough to get us to Birmingham in time.

The only conversation I remember came when Mary said, "You've got to let me drive. You'll be dead."

"I'll be all right. I want to get there."

"Why?"

"So I can play tonight."

"They don't expect you tonight. Take it easy."

"I can't take it easy," I said. "I've *got* to get there in time for the game."

We pulled into Birmingham at about eight o'clock that night. I dropped Mary and Eileen off at the hotel, left her to check us in and dashed for the ball park. By the time I was in uniform, the game had started.

Red Marion, the Barons manager, was amazed when I walked into the dugout.

"What did you do — fly?" he asked, shaking hands.

"No, I drove. How's for putting me in the game?"

"You drove? All the way from Louisville?"

"Sure. Hey, Red, can't I play?"

"Next inning," he said. "Soon as we get up."

I went in as a pinch hitter and slapped the first pitch to right center field. The ball landed safely, and I thought I could make three bases on it. As I approached third, the coach gave me the sign to slide. I hit the dirt.

"You're out!" yelled the umpire. Then, as the dust cleared away, he said, "Hi, Jim! Didn't know you were in town."

It was Augie Guglielmo, a Waterbury boy whom I knew well. He used to umpire a lot of our games when I played for the Insilcos.

"Just got in," I said. "Was it close?"

"Nah. You were out a mile."

That was the beginning of one of the greatest baseball seasons I've ever had. Marion, a tall, skinny, easygoing guy, put me out in center field and let me do pretty much as I pleased. Red's brother, Marty, the Cardinals' famed "Mr. Shortstop" in his playing days, now manages the Chicago White Sox. The two don't look much alike, but their temperaments are similar. No matter what happens, neither one gets excited or upset. All Red ever had to do was give me an occasional pat on the back and tell me how good I was and I wanted to break my neck for him.

I hit .346 and came close to leading the league in batting. More important, I slammed fifteen home runs, pulling the ball to left field several times, and I led all the outfielders in putouts and assists, even though I didn't get started until three weeks after the Southern Association season began.

"You can't miss," Marion said. "You're a big leaguer right now."

In August, Johnny Murphy, the Red Sox farm director, stopped by in Birmingham for what appeared to be
a routine visit. I didn't know Murphy very well, although
I had met him a number of times. A big man with a huge
square jaw and Irish blue eyes, he once starred for the
New York Yankees, where he was known as "Grandma"
Murphy because he swayed back and forth as if he were
in a rocking chair when he wound up to pitch. Murphy
was baseball's best relief pitcher for years. He was a soft-
spoken man who did a great deal more thinking than
talking. He had little to say, but every phrase was worth
listening to. He doled out each word as if he figured
there were only so many to a lifetime and he didn't want
to waste one on trivialities. Johnny never talked just to
pass the time of day.

He pulled me aside one day and said, "You handle
ground balls well, and you've got a fine arm. Why don't
you fool around in the infield a little before games?"

If I had known Murphy better, I would have realized
that there was a method in his madness. But the suggestion made no particular impression on me. Some outfielders tried to improve their handling of ground balls by
working with the infielders during practice, and I thought
that was why Murphy wanted me to do it. So, every day,
after I had chased fly balls in the outfield for a while, I
moved into the infield, where grounders came hot off
the bat. Anyone who could field one in the infield would
certainly have little trouble scooping one up in the outfield, where most ground balls, their speed spent, roll
much more slowly.

I was grateful to Murphy for making the suggestion, for I had never thought of working with the infielders. After a while, I found that it wasn't too hard getting grounders and hard bouncing balls, and I rather enjoyed it. I wouldn't have wanted it as a steady diet, of course, but I knew the experience would help me in my outfield play.

The Barons finished second in the Southern Association standing, but then we won the league playoffs, which put us into the Dixie Series. This is a sort of Southern World Series, with the winner of the Southern Association playoffs meeting the winner of the Texas League playoffs, which were won by the Houston Buffs that year.

We beat the Buffs, four games out of six, and I was the star of the series. I made several spectacular plays and piled up an impressive .476 batting average, which was even more important to me, since I was expected to field well anyhow. I led both teams in batting for the series. When it was over, I was sitting on top of the world.

Williams, DiMaggio — and Piersall! What an outfield! Now it's less than a year away.

I hurried to Scranton by air. Mary and Eileen had driven home in the car a month ahead of time, since Mary's sister Ann, who had been with us all summer, had to get back in time for school. My dad came down to watch the Dixie Series, and he and I flew as far as New York together. Since we were no longer living together, we got along better than we ever had before. He recognized me as an equal and he never raised his voice or showed any signs of annoyance.

We settled down with Mary's father in his house at the corner of Capouse Avenue and Woodlawn Street in Scranton. Life looked wonderful to me. I had had that marvelous season in Birmingham, there was a little money in the bank and I was almost a sure shot to stick with the Red Sox — and play regularly — in 1952. Mary was expecting a new baby in the spring, and she seemed to be taking it in stride. All I had to do was get a job for the winter, and everything would be fine.

By this time I was pretty well known in Scranton so I figured I would have no trouble finding something to do. I loafed around the house for a week, then called up a few people I knew to see what sort of work I could get. Nobody was particularly discouraging, so I started out confident that there would be no snags.

I didn't have any trouble getting to see people, but jobs turned out to be scarce. Scranton is practically a one-industry city. When things go well in the mines, they go well everywhere. That winter, the mines were slow, and the economy all over town was affected. There not only weren't any part-time jobs in Scranton; there weren't any full-time jobs either. On the contrary, people were being fired left and right. Even George, my father-in-law, who was rarely out of work, was expecting to be laid off any day.

The days became weeks, and I still couldn't find a job. Now a whole new cluster of worries loomed to plague my days and harry my nights. My Red Sox bonus money was all used up, and I would collect no more from the ball club until my salary began when the 1952 season opened.

[92]

I would get the big-league minimum of six thousand dollars, but that wasn't doing me any good in November of 1951. I still had to send my parents thirty-five dollars a week, and that was beginning to make a serious dent in my pocketbook.

Now it's almost Thanksgiving and I still haven't got a job. It doesn't look as if I'm going to get one either. What will Mom and Dad do if I have to stop sending them money? And how much longer can I send them anything? There's nothing coming in. What about Mary and Eileen — and the new baby? What if Mary should get sick again? She was so sick before! How do I know it won't happen again? And how about Mom? She's been all right, but will she always be? What if Dad should have another heart attack? Mary's dad can help if we want him to, but he has obligations of his own. Besides, he might lose his job any day.

Panic was setting in again, but Mary knew the signs now. One day she said, "Honey, why don't you start going to the gym again? You can play some basketball and work out, and get yourself into good physical condition."

"I don't want to waste any time," I replied. "I ought to be out looking for a job."

"There aren't any jobs this year. There won't be any now. I know this town. But we've got money in the bank, honey. We'll live on that."

I felt better after I began going to the gym. It helped, if for no other reason than that it gave me something to do and somewhere to go every day. Until I started working out there, I was doing nothing but mope around the house. Now I played basketball and pulled on weights and did calisthenics, and, what with one thing or another, I managed to work off some of the tension.

One day, about two weeks before Christmas, I was sitting on the porch, idly leafing through the December 12 issue of the *Sporting News,* the weekly newspaper that is known in sports circles everywhere as baseball's Bible. The *Sporting News* carries weekly dispatches about all of the major-league clubs throughout the year, both in and out of season, and I don't know of any ballplayer who doesn't read it, particularly during the winter, when the daily newspapers carry very little about baseball.

I found the dispatch about the Red Sox near the back of the paper. The story was a routine discussion of Vern Stephens, the club's shortstop, who had been having trouble with one hip. Lou Boudreau, who had succeeded Steve O'Neill as manager of the club, was quoted at great length on the subject of Stephens. As usual, I read the story through, never expecting to find my own name in it. But suddenly the printed page seemed to leap up and crack me right across the face. This is what it said:

"One planned move is the converting of Jimmy Piersall, minor-league outfielding sensation with Birmingham last season, into a shortstop. Piersall will be the chief target of the Red Sox brass at the special training camp which opens in Sarasota January 15."

Shortstop! Me? I stared, unbelieving, through rapidly misting eyes. *What were these people thinking of? I wasn't a shortstop. I'd never be a shortstop.* Somehow, I made myself read on.

" 'We may be able to turn him into a top-notch short-stop,' Boudreau said. 'The kid has great natural instinct on ground balls.' "

Natural instinct, my foot! Maybe I had natural instinct on fly balls, but not on ground balls. What's this guy Boudreau talking about?

"Boudreau will tutor Piersall personally at the special training session," the story went on. "The manager him-self will decide whether or not the youngster has a future as a shortstop.

" 'If he does,' Boudreau said, 'I'll farm him out a year. I'd never take him up as a shortstop right off.' "

It's impossible! I'm not a shortstop. I'm a center fielder, the best center fielder in the American League. Dominic DiMaggio himself had told me that. They can't be planning to shift me now! It doesn't make sense. What makes them think they can make a shortstop out of me? Just trying to shift from the outfield might ruin me.

Ruin me? Wait a minute. I'll bet that's just what they want to do. They know that if I'm going to stay with the Red Sox, it has to be as an outfielder. But they want out-fielders who can pull the ball to left field — guys like Karl Olson. O.K. And they know I'll never be a big-league shortstop. That's pretty obvious. Look what Boudreau said — it's right there in the Sporting News. *He said if it looked as if I could make the club as a shortstop, he'd farm me out for a year. That means I'm damned if I do and damned if I don't. If I look good as a shortstop, I'll go to the minors. If I look bad, I'll go to the minors any-way.*

[95]

Now everything slides into its proper place like pieces in a jigsaw puzzle. The Red Sox don't want me at all, and this is their way of brushing me off. All I have to do is think back — it's all as plain as day. First O'Neill made me sit on the Red Sox bench. He put his arm around me and told me how good I was going to be some day, but he didn't mean a word of it. He knew I couldn't stand being on the bench. He knew that sooner or later I'd ask to be sent out somewhere. He had this all planned out — either he or somebody higher up in the Red Sox outfit had it planned out. Anyhow, getting me away from the Red Sox was the first step.

Then look what happened. They sent me to Louisville, where they knew I wasn't wanted. Higgins had his line-up all planned, and it didn't include me. Sure, he went through the motions of playing me for a couple of weeks, but then he benched me. Higgins knew that was the quickest way to get rid of me. It had worked for O'Neill in Boston and it was bound to work for him in Louisville. It did, of course. When I told Doherty I wanted to go elsewhere, I was playing right into their hands. Getting me away from the Colonels was the second step.

And where was my good friend Doherty all this time? He was Higgins's boss. He could have ordered Higgins to play me. But he didn't. Instead, what did my wonderful pal Doherty do? He sent me to Birmingham, that's what. He didn't lift a finger to help me in Louisville.

Well, they thought I'd get discouraged and quit when I got sent down to the Southern Association, but I fooled 'em. I had such a good season that they had to carry things further. They had to send Murphy to Birmingham to tell me to work out in the infield. Oh, but that Murphy was shrewd! "You've got a fine arm," he said. "You handle ground balls well," he said. "Why don't you fool around a little in the infield?" he said. Sure I'll fool around in the infield. It'll finish me, but I'll do it — and fall right into their trap. Sending Murphy down there to tell me to fool around in the infield was the third step.

And now here's the fourth step, the crusher — Boudreau, the new manager, announcing that he's going to shift me to shortstop. He knows I read the Sporting News. *He made that announcement just for my benefit. He knows I'll never be a big-league shortstop. The Red Sox don't want me. Why, their whole organization has ganged up on me!*

I don't know how long I sat on George's porch in Scranton, staring sightlessly at the *Sporting News*. It might have been ten minutes or it might have been an hour. I saw nothing, heard nothing and was aware of nothing but my thoughts until, as if from a long distance away, I heard my name being called.

"Jimmy! Jimmy, honey! What's the matter? You look as if you've seen a ghost."

It was Mary, crouched in front of me, her hand on my shoulder, her eyes brimming, her forehead wrinkled.

"What's wrong, dear? What happened?"

"Nothing, honey. Not a thing. I'm just through, that's all."

"Through? What do you mean, through?"

"The Red Sox don't want me." I pointed to the paper on my lap.

"Don't want you? Did they trade you?" she asked.

"No — they didn't trade me."

"Then how do you know they don't want you?"

"Look — read it — right down here — see?"

I pointed to a paragraph about me, and Mary read it rapidly. Then, with a long, low sigh, she looked at me and smiled.

"Why, honey, that's wonderful!" she exclaimed. "They're going to need a shortstop and they've picked you. You'll be trained by Boudreau personally — and he was one of the best shortstops in the business. Why, they're making a place especially for you."

"Mary —" I tried to talk slowly, like a patient parent about to explain a tragic event to an innocent child. "You don't understand at all. This isn't wonderful. This is a brush-off. They want to get rid of me, but they can't just drop me. Instead, they're using this means of getting me to quit. That's how they got me away from Boston last spring and that's how they got me out of Louisville. They thought I'd fall apart in Birmingham, but instead I had the best year of my life. When they saw what was happening, they sent Murphy down to get me to work with the infielders, and now they're going to make me do something they know I can't do. They're going to shift me to shortstop knowing that I'll never make it. Then, they figure, I'll quit and they'll be rid of me. Can't you see that, Mary?"

[98]

She looked at me for a long time. Then she reached out with one hand and gently stroked my cheek. I thought her mouth quivered a little, but I couldn't be sure. All I knew was that I loved her very much and her hand felt cool and I wished I could make her understand.

At last she said, "Jimmy, honey, I'm sure you're wrong, but let's not talk about it now any more. You just keep right on going to the gym to work out and stay in shape, and then when they order you to the special training camp in January, you go on down and do what they tell you."

She didn't understand it at all. She's like an ostrich. She's got her head buried in the sand so she can't see what she doesn't want to see. I'm not going to the gym any more and I'm not going to that special training camp in January. But why bring it up now? It will only cause an argument.

The next morning I took my basketball shoes and shorts, kissed Mary and the baby good-by and started down the street in the direction of the gym, but I never got there. As soon as I turned the corner and was out of Mary's sight, I headed towards a downtown movie house which opened early in the day. I didn't take a direct route, because that would have involved walking along the main thoroughfare. Instead, I ducked through back streets and alleys, approaching the theater from a side street, so that I had to walk only a few feet on the crowded avenue. I looked furtively around, to make sure no one I knew was watching me, then bought a ticket and stepped into the movie.

The place was nearly empty — it was still an hour before noon — but I tiptoed my way down the aisle. I didn't want to sit too far back because I might be seen by people first coming in, and I didn't want to be on an aisle for the same reason. I picked a spot right in the middle of the theater, moved in, sat down and idly watched the picture. I don't remember what it was about even though I saw it through three times. I wasn't interested in the picture. All I wanted to do was hide.

I sat in the theater all day, and didn't walk out until I was certain it was dark outside. Then I started back for the house, using the same devious route I had taken that morning. It was about seven o'clock by this time — I would be only a little late for dinner. When I walked into the house, Mary greeted me with a kiss and said, "How was it?"

"All right," I replied, vaguely.

"Did you have a good workout?"

"Yeah — real good."

"You must have taken a stiff one," she said. "You're late for dinner."

"I'm sorry, hon."

"That's all right. Sit down and eat. Oh, by the way, want a canasta game tonight? Ann and Dan are coming over."

Ann O'Brien and Dan Kuchar, who were going to be married soon, were among our closest friends. I was fond of them both and liked to play cards with them. But I said, "Mary, tell them not to come."

"What's the matter? Don't you want to see them?"

"Uh — it isn't that. I'm tired, that's all."

"They won't stay late," Mary said.

"I'm tired, I tell you. I don't want to see them. Understand?"

"Yes, I understand. I'll phone them."

That night I went to bed with a terrific headache, one of the worst I had ever suffered. I lay in bed, twisting and turning and muttering to myself. Suddenly, Eileen woke up and started to cry. She had been sick off and on all fall. I always got up in the night because I usually was awake anyhow. Besides, I wanted Mary to sleep so she would have no complications. She had to get up early enough in the morning as it was.

For one stretch of three weeks, Eileen was up every single night, and I got so I couldn't stand hearing her cry. When she woke up this time, I didn't go to her. Instead, I buried my head under the pillow and muttered over and over, "Stop that howling — stop that howling — stop that howling —" I guess I said it aloud, because Mary finally woke up and, without a word, went in to Eileen. After a while, the baby quieted down. I turned over and acted as if I were asleep when Mary came back to bed. Feeling guilty and conscience-stricken, I didn't want to talk.

Every day after that, I went through the same routine — kissing Mary good-by, heading in the direction of the gym and ending up in a movie. Sometimes I'd go to the same theater two or three days in a row, sometimes I'd switch off to some other movie. Sometimes I'd go to one in town, sometimes to a suburban house. This went on through Christmas week, and I thought I had Mary pretty completely fooled.

One day she said, "Here's a letter for you. It's from the Red Sox."

It was short, hardly more than a note, signed by Joe Cronin, the Red Sox general manager, an invitation — not an order — for me to report on January 15 to Sarasota for a series of workouts in the special spring-training school the club was running. The school would be made up mostly of young rookies like myself. The Red Sox had so many that they had decided to give the boys a chance to get a head start on the veterans, who weren't due to report for regular spring training until March 1.

"I'm not going," I said, shortly.

"Well," Mary commented, "I don't suppose you have to if you don't want to. But you'll be way behind the other fellows if you don't go."

"What do the Red Sox care? They don't want me."

I stayed in the movies later than usual the following night. When I got home — it was after nine — Tony Howley was at the house.

"Hi, Jimmy," he said. "Where've you been?"

"Around."

I hadn't seen Tony for days. I had been avoiding everyone I knew.

"How were the movies?" he said, casually.

"The what?"

"The movies. Saw you there today."

"Uh — all right." Then, to Mary, "I didn't feel like working out today, honey."

"Jimmy," she said, slowly, "you haven't felt like working out for a long time, have you?"

"What makes you say that?"

"You haven't been fooling me, honey, but it's all right. If it makes you feel any better to go to the movies every day, go ahead. But it's pretty nearly time to report to Florida, and you haven't been sleeping too well. Tony's got an idea he might be able to help you."

So she knew all the time — and she hadn't said a word. But now Tony knew, too. Why had she told him? It was none of his business. But he wants to help me. Maybe I can use some help. I've got to get some sleep. Maybe it will stop these headaches.

"— you'll like him," Tony was saying.

"Like who?" I asked.

"This doctor I was telling you about."

"You didn't tell me about any doctor."

"You weren't listening, Jimmy. This is a guy who can give you something to make you sleep."

"What kind of a doctor is he?" I asked, suspiciously.

"Just an ordinary doctor. Mary knows him."

"Who is he?" I asked her.

"A good man," she said. "I'm going to make an appointment for you to see him before you go South."

"I don't need a doctor," I said sullenly. But I wanted to get rid of the headaches and, after a while, I agreed to go.

Mary made an appointment for the next afternoon. I stayed home all day, prowling around the house, playing with Eileen, trying to read the papers, killing time any way I could. When Mary said, "O.K., let's go," I helped her into a coat, put one on myself and went out to the car.

It took us only a few minutes to get to the doctor's. He

saw me right away, and, while Mary sat in the waiting room, I walked into the office. As soon as I got inside, I snapped, "This wasn't my idea. My wife wanted me to see you."

"That's all right," he commented. "Just sit down."

"I won't be here long. I'll stand. Just give me something that'll make me sleep."

"I'd like to ask you one or two questions — then I'll give you something."

While I walked back and forth in front of him, he began talking, but I hardly listened. Instead, I kept repeating, "O.K., O.K., just give me the sleeping pills." Finally, unable to stand his voice any longer, I turned and walked out. I picked up my coat and said to Mary, "Come on. We're getting out of here."

A few nights before it was time to leave for Sarasota — I had steadily insisted that I wasn't going — Mary drove the car up beside me as I was walking along Capouse Avenue, about three blocks from the house. As usual I had spent the day in the movies.

"It's after ten, Jimmy," she said, calmly, as she leaned out. "Time to come home."

The thermometer was flirting with zero, but I dripped with perspiration as I crunched through the snow. Cold as it was, I had my coat unbuttoned and the collar of my shirt open. My head buzzed with the pressure of pain and my eyes smarted. I was staring at the ground as I walked along, but now I looked up. Then, without a word, I climbed into the car and Mary drove us home. My dad was waiting for me when we got there.

"Hello, son."

His harsh voice was pitched low, and he had an odd smile on his face.

"What are you doing here?" I managed to ask. I couldn't say any more. My throat was tight and my shoulders were quivering and my eyes were smarting more than ever. I sank down on the divan, cradled my pounding head in my arms and cried like a baby.

After a while, I heard Dad say, "All set to go South?"

"I'm not going," I sobbed. "They don't want me."

"Sure they want you. Say, Jimmy, you know who was asking for you yesterday? Bill Tracy. He read that you were invited to that rookie school, and he can't wait to see how you do."

"I won't be there."

"Jimmy —"

My dad's voice was very soft now, softer than I ever remembered it.

"Yeah?"

"Tracy'd like to see you."

Tracy wants to see me? Good old Tracy. Such a decent, fair, straight-shooting guy! He knows me and understands me like nobody else does — even Mary. He's the only person I know I can trust. He's my friend. He'll tell me what to do.

"I'd like to see him, too," I said.

"Fine. We'll go to Waterbury in the morning."

Bill met us at the railroad station and drove us over to East Main Street so I could say hello to Mom. We dropped my father off, and then went back to Tracy's house, where

[105]

we talked for a while. He told me that no one was trying to get rid of me — that the Red Sox needed me as short-stop and were giving me a chance to play one position that was almost sure to be open right away.

"Just because Boudreau announced that he wouldn't bring you into the majors now if you look like a promising shortstop doesn't mean that he really won't," Bill explained. "If you look that good, you'll stay right with the team. He can't get rid of you, because he doesn't have another shortstop. Stephens's hip is still doubtful. There isn't anyone else."

"I know, but look at the way I got pushed around last year."

"You didn't get pushed around, Jim," he said. "You pushed yourself around. It all started when you asked O'Neill to send you down."

It didn't sound right to me, but Bill seemed to know what he was talking about. He failed to convince me that the Red Sox really wanted me, but I did agree to report to the special training camp just to see what would happen. I took a late afternoon train back to Scranton. It was January 13. I had less than forty-eight hours to get to Sarasota.

I got home late, then paced the floor for a couple of hours before I went to bed. *I don't want to go to Sarasota. I'll get pushed around some more there. The Red Sox don't like me and they don't want me. But I'll go — I promised Tracy I would, and I can't let Tracy down. Besides, I want to prove to him how wrong he is. He thinks Boudreau will keep me with the Red Sox. Of course, he's wrong. Boudreau will make me fool around in the infield awhile and then send me back to Louisville, or maybe Birmingham, and that's the last I'll ever see of the Red Sox. Bill Tracy's a smart guy, but he doesn't know all the answers. I'll go. I told him I'd go. But I'll fool him and Boudreau and everyone else. I'll go down there without my fielder's glove! That'll stop everyone. You can't work out without a glove. I didn't tell Tracy I'd work out. I just promised him I'd report to the ball club in time to make the special training school. When they see that I don't have my glove, they'll know I mean business. Yes, sir, I'll leave my glove home.*

I felt better. The headache was still bad, but I could lie down and rest, if not sleep. It was now after three o'clock in the morning. Mary had stayed up to see me after I got in from Scranton, but she had long since gone to sleep. Eileen seemed to be all right. There wasn't a peep out of her. I couldn't have stood it if she had waked up and cried.

After a miserable night, I got up and took an ice-cold shower. Then after she had given me some breakfast, Mary said, "Come on. Let's go down to the airlines' office and get your ticket. You have to be in Sarasota by to-morrow."

She had one hand on my shoulder. I reached up and touched it and, for a minute, I felt relaxed.

"How do you feel, honey?" I asked her.

"Fine."

"You know, I've been so upset myself, I forgot all about you for a little while. Take care of yourself?"

"I will, Jimmy."

"We don't want anything to happen this time."

"Don't worry. Nothing will. It'll be just like when we had Eileen. Nice and routine."

"I *will* worry."

"You've got enough on your mind, honey," she said. "You just go down there to Florida and show all those people that you're a big-league ballplayer, and don't think about me. I'll be all right."

"Mary —"

"What?"

"I'm not a big-league ballplayer — not if they try to make a shortstop out of me."

"How do you know? You've never tried to play shortstop. Jimmy, honey, the Red Sox know what they're doing. They wouldn't try to shift you if they didn't think you could do it."

I didn't say anything. *What's the use of starting another argument? Mary doesn't understand, and she never will understand. I'll just go along with her, and even act as if I agree. What's the difference? I won't have my glove with me, so I can't possibly practice. But she doesn't know that. She never will know. If she asks me about it later, I'll tell her I lost it.*

Mary helped me pack the old foot locker — the same one I had first taken to Bradenton — and we sent it on ahead by air express when we went down to pick up my plane ticket. After we arrived back at the house, she said, "Now get out your two-suiter and we'll pack it."

"I'll pack it," I told her.

"You go and take it easy, honey. You've got a tough trip ahead."

"I'll pack it, I said," I blazed.

Mary, her eyes wide, backed away a few steps.

"All right, Jimmy. Pack it if you want. I just thought I could help you."

"I don't need any help," I said, sullenly.

If Mary packs it, she'll be sure I take the glove and if I take the glove I won't have any excuse not to work out. I've got to leave the glove behind. I'll hide it in my bureau drawer. She won't think to look for it there. I'll dump everything else into the suitcase and get it closed and locked before she comes back into the room. She'll never know the difference.

I pulled the two-suiter off the closet shelf, spread it open on the bed and threw my clothes into it. I worked fast, and the job didn't take long. I snapped the clasp shut, turned the key in the little lock, then put the key in my pocket. I breathed a long sigh. Mary hadn't come into the room at all. *Good. Very good. No glove, no workout. Now I'm just going to Sarasota for the ride.*

My plane was scheduled to leave at nine-thirty P.M., and, as Mary had pointed out, it would not be an easy trip. I'd either be flying or hanging around airports all night, since I'd have to make two changes, one in New York, the other in Tampa. Shortly after dinner, Mary, George and I got into George's car, drove in town to pick up Tony and Bob Howley and then went out to the Scranton–Wilkes-Barre airport.

I felt good. My head only ached a little and I wasn't too

nervous. The conversation was pretty general, and I took part in it. *I won't have to talk to anybody once the plane starts. I don't want to talk to anybody — not ever again. I hope I don't meet anyone I know. Meanwhile, I might as well be nice to everyone here.*

When the flight was called, I shook hands with the Howleys and George, kissed Mary and started for the plane. I took only a few steps, then remembered something. Turning back, I beckoned to Mary, and she stepped towards me. When we met, I put my arms around her, kissed her again and murmured, "Take care of yourself, honey."

She smiled, a warm, happy smile, then replied, softly, "Don't worry, I will."

The new baby was due in six weeks.

I climbed aboard the plane, nodded an acknowledgment to the stewardess's greeting and walked the length of the aisle, taking a rear seat beside the window. I fastened the safety belt, pulled my hat down over my face, leaned my head against the window and half closed my eyes. I made no attempt to go to sleep, because it is only a short plane ride from Scranton to New York and I had the whole night in front of me.

At LaGuardia, I had about an hour's wait for the Tampa plane, which was scheduled to take off a little after midnight. I prowled back and forth on the long straight corridor that leads to the plane gates, hoping to tire myself out enough so that I'd be able to sleep on the long ride south. My head was buzzing again. I hadn't had a real night's sleep in weeks, and the last thirty hours had been a nightmare. By the time the Tampa flight was called, I was ready to drop. I picked up my grip and stumbled aboard the plane, falling into the first window seat I came to. I fastened the belt and cradled my head into the corner formed by the casement and the back of the seat and I must have gone to sleep before the plane took off. When I woke up, we were taxiing along the ground in Tampa. My seat belt was still fastened.

The airstrip gleamed in the morning sun, and my winter clothes felt itchy and heavy as I stepped off the plane. In spite of the long sleep, I was jumpy and uncomfortable, and the band of pain was tight across my forehead. I washed up and had a cup of coffee, but the headache persisted. By now I had about three quarters of an hour to kill before the Sarasota plane would be ready. I went into a far corner of the waiting room and sat down, turning my head so that no one could get a clear view of me.

Oh, God, why won't the Red Sox leave me alone? I want to be a big-league ballplayer and I'm good enough to be a big-league ballplayer if they'd let me. What did I ever do to make them treat me this way? If they don't want me to play the outfield for them, why don't they trade me? Nobody in the whole outfit has any use for me. Why? What started all this? And why do they have to go through such a complicated arrangement to make me quit? Why do they have to go through this farce of announcing that I was going to be a shortstop? They know I'll never make it, so why doesn't somebody just pull me aside and say, "Look, Jimmy, you don't belong here with us. We're going to let you go"?

Well, maybe they'll do it now. I can't practice without a glove. Lucky Mary didn't pack my two-suiter. She'd have put the glove into it, and I wouldn't have had any excuse not to work out. I'd have had to hang around Sarasota. This way, I can tell them I have no glove, then turn around and go home. That'll be better for me. Why wait for the Red Sox to tell me to go? I'll leave of my own accord.

The Sarasota plane was called. Mechanically, I stood up and, keeping my head down, walked towards the gate. *There might be other ballplayers here. I don't want any of them to see me. If someone recognizes me, he'll come over and talk to me and I don't want to talk to anyone.* Head down, hat pulled over my eyes, I went up the steps and into the plane. I left the suitcase in the luggage compartment and walked the length of the plane. *Thank goodness, there's nobody in that last window seat.* I strapped myself in and looked out into the bright sunlight.

The motors turned over, and the plane shook with the vibration, then taxied out to the runway. I didn't dare look away from the window. There was no one sitting beside me, but I didn't know who might be across the aisle. *There must be ballplayers aboard. Please, God, don't let any of them see me.*

It's barely half an hour by air from Tampa to the Sarasota-Bradenton airport, with a stop at St. Petersburg in between. When we arrived at Sarasota, I sat still until all the passengers who were going there were off the plane. Then I stood up and, without looking up, moved through the plane. After getting my grip, I carefully walked down the steps, moved through the waiting room and got into a rear seat of the Sarasota limousine. I kept my head down the whole time. When it was necessary to look to see where I was going, I raised only my eyes.

Now I mustn't be seen. This is the last leg of the trip. The next stop will be the hotel. I mustn't talk. I mustn't be recognized. I mustn't let anyone know I'm here — not in the limousine. I mustn't look up. I may catch the eye of someone who knows me, and I can't stand that.

I was dimly aware of a clattering headache, much worse than usual, and my hands were clammy with sweat. There were butterflies in my stomach and the tension seemed unbearable as we approached the Sarasota-Terrace Hotel. The blood was pounding through my veins and my nerves seemed to whine aloud for release.

Why am I so nervous? I know exactly what I'm going to do. I'll check in and go upstairs to my room. I won't talk to anyone except maybe my roommate. I'll have a roommate, of course. Maybe he won't be in yet. Then pretty soon, I'll get a call, maybe from Boudreau or one of the coaches, and they'll tell me what time to report to Payne Field. I hope it's this afternoon, so I can get this all over with. I'll be given a uniform, and I'll get into it. The boys will be pretty quiet this first day, so nobody will notice that I'm not talking to anyone. After a while, we'll go out on the field. Then Boudreau will say, "O.K., Piersall, you go to shortstop." And I'll say, "But I don't have a glove. How can I go to shortstop?" And he'll say, "No glove? Then you can't work, can you?" And I'll say, "No, I can't work." And he'll say, "Well, you might as well go

[113]

home then." And I'll say, "I might as well." And he'll say,
"We really don't want you anyhow. This business of shift-
ing you to shortstop was just to let you know we don't
want you around." And I'll say, "Thanks for being
honest." And that will be that.

Now we were in front of the hotel, and I was backing
out of the limousine, crablike, so that I wouldn't be recognized by anyone who might be sitting in the hotel patio.
I stood aside, facing the big car, while the driver dug my
two-suiter out of the trunk. My heart was beating a frantic tattoo on my ribs and my head was splitting and my
eyes were smarting, and the winter suit hung heavy on
my saturated shoulders. My muscles ached and my mouth
was dry and my throat burned and my whole body was
being pulled every which way by a thousand frenetic nerve
ends restlessly straining and tugging and tumbling all
over each other.

I paid the driver, picked up my suitcase and turned
towards the hotel. I moved slowly, like a man on a tread-
mill, and headed for the front door.

Head down — head down — there are people on the
patio. Some of them have to be ballplayers. They'll see
you and recognize you and say something. Don't answer
them. Head down —

Without looking in either direction, without even rais-
ing my eyes, I crossed the patio and stepped over the
threshold. Then I began walking across the lobby. . . .

WHEN you look out the window of the violent room in the Westborough State Hospital, your eye first catches sight of a huge water tower, which is set high on a hill and dominates everything around it. The tower is close by the hospital and perhaps a mile in from the Worcester Turnpike, one of the main highways leading south and west from Boston. I drive over that road often in the wintertime, and whenever I pass the water tower, I say a prayer. I pray for Mary and I pray for the children and I pray for all the people who still must see the water tower only from that other angle and, most of all, I pray that it will never again happen to me.

How many prayers have I whispered as I looked out the windows of the violent room! How many times have I repeated the Rosary in the shadows of that tower! How often have I fixed my mind on prayers to God and St. Joseph and St. Anthony while I fixed my eyes on the tower outside! St. Joseph, patron saint of the family unit, is my favorite. St. Anthony, my name saint, is patron saint for the recovery of lost objects — and I had been on the very edge of losing everything.

That water tower was my friend while I was struggling back from oblivion and it is still my friend, the symbol of prayer and hope and all the things that helped me in my successful battle to recover my wits and banish the fears that had sent me so closely within its sight. When I see it from the highway, it reminds me not of Westborough and the violent room and the old trouble, but of prayers that were answered to a degree far beyond my happiest dreams. When I pass it today, I feel spiritually refreshed and mentally relaxed.

My first memory of Westborough was a flood of sunshine, streaming in from the window facing the water tower and so bright that I tried to shade my eyes with my hand. But I couldn't reach up, so I turned my head away. I tried again to cover my eyes with my hands, but I could only move from the neck up. I was securely strapped to a bed, and a man I never remembered seeing before was peering thoughtfully at me. When I focused my eyes on him, he said, kindly, "Time to eat."

I tried to struggle up to one elbow, but the straps were tight.

"Where am I?" I asked.

"In a hospital."

"What kind of a hospital?"

"You've been a very sick boy."

"What am I doing here? How long have I been here? How long will I have to stay?"

"I don't know," the man said. "I'll get the doctor."

"Who are you?"

"An attendant. I can't tell you anything."

He moved off, and I twisted my head so that I could see part of the room. I was in a sort of alcove, off what appeared to be a fairly good-sized ward. There were about fifteen or twenty men there, some walking rather aimlessly back and forth and others, like me, in similar alcoves strapped down — or at least I presumed that was the case, because I could only see the alcove opposite mine. A few were eating from trays set on a table in the middle of the room. No one spoke.

Suddenly, I was startled to hear a weird, blood-curdling shriek — a piercing, raucous, spine-shuddering animal sound so frightening that my body stiffened in sheer horror. One of the men who had been walking about the room began alternately waving his arms around and tearing at his hair and his clothes, while he broke into a dead run. He crashed into one wall, staggered back, then, like an ant, turned instinctively in another direction. His shrieking, punctuated by an occasional, plainly discernible, "Let me out of here!" continued for what seemed like hours.

Actually, he was overpowered before he could smash himself against another side of the wall. Four or five attendants, including the one who had been standing by my bed, rushed him and, after a brief struggle, took him off to one side, beyond my own sphere of vision. I heard him whimpering for a while and then, finally, evidently strapped down on a bed in one of the other alcoves, he quieted down.

Oh, God, was I that way? Did I run in circles and wave my arms and tear my hair and scream and smash into walls? Did I have these other guys looking at me with dead eyes — or recoiling as I just recoiled when I saw what this man was doing? Why, I must have! Otherwise, I wouldn't be strapped down like this. That attendant was right. I've been a sick boy.

I turned my head away from the room and back to-

[117]

wards the window, and for the first time I noticed the water tower. There it stood, high and solid, almost majestic, and, more than anything else, normal. *What can be more normal, more commonplace, than a water tower? That's what I want to be — normal and commonplace — an average guy. I don't ever again want to be different.*

I closed my eyes and clenched my fists and prayed — hard. "Please, God," I murmured, "make me well and normal so I can get out of here soon, and let me play ball so I can take care of my family. I don't know how I got here or how long I've stayed, but make the rest of the time short." I prayed for five minutes or so, to God, to Jesus, to St. Joseph, to St. Anthony, and then I opened my eyes. I felt someone loosening my straps and, turning my head back, saw that another stranger was standing by my bed.

He smiled when our eyes met, and I managed a weak smile. *Who is this man? I know him — I'm sure I do. Where have I seen him before?*

Then he spoke, in a soft Latin-American accent, and I was sure I knew him. He was of medium height, with jet-black curly hair. His eyes were deep brown and his features were handsomely regular. He had a short, straight nose, his mouth was wide, his chin firm and he had the whitest teeth I ever saw.

"How do you feel?" he asked, his voice pitched low.

"I'm all right. How long have I been here?"

"Two weeks, give or take a day."

"How much longer will I have to stay?"

He shrugged.

"That's up to you."

I stared at him. Then, sitting up, I snapped my fingers and exclaimed, "Say, you're not — you can't be — that television guy — Desi Arnaz. That's who you are. What are you doing here, of all places?"

"Well, to begin with, I'm not Desi Arnaz."

"Then you must be his twin brother."

"No," he said, "I'm not even related to him. But I guess I look like him. I've been approached in railroad stations and airports and hotel lobbies and streetcar stops and parties and everywhere else you can think of by people asking for my autograph. You must know how it feels to be hounded by autograph hunters."

"It's wonderful. I wish — I hope — how soon will it be before people will be after me again?"

"Not long — if you do what we want you to."

"I will — and who are you?"

"I'm Dr. Brown — Guillermo Brown. My home is in Mexico. I'm a resident physician here."

I held out my hand, and he shook it.

"My name's Jimmy Piersall."

"I know."

"Now tell me — please. Where am I and what kind of a hospital is this and what kind of a room am I in and what kind of a doctor are you?"

"You are in the Westborough State Hospital," he said, "a mental institution. This is the violent room. I'm a psy-chiatrist."

"Then I've been —"

"— sick. But you're getting well. In a little while —

later this afternoon, we'll have a talk. I'll be back in an hour or so."

In the next few weeks, Dr. Brown became friend, adviser and confidant, a willing repository for all my hopes and fears and ambitions and dreams, a spiritual sponge that sopped up the core of my conscious and subconscious mind. We talked every day, sometimes for hours at a time, or rather, I suppose I should say I talked and he listened. A key question here, a nod there, sometimes only a smile, was all I needed from him to get me going. He drew out everything — the good and the bad — and he grew to know me as no one except Mary has ever known me before or since.

The first question he asked when he returned later the day I came to my senses was, "Do you know that you have been sick?"

"I know now," I replied.

"Good. Very good. It is very important that you admit you were sick."

"I feel all right now."

"I'm sure that you are all right," the doctor said. "You'll be out of here soon. But you must co-operate. Do as you're told and everything will work out."

"Doc," I said suddenly, "what month is it?"

"August."

"August?"

"You may have lost a little time, Jimmy. Don't think about it now."

I shook my head, slowly. Then I said, "All right. If you say so."

I woke up the next morning, feeling calm and refreshed and relaxed, and it wasn't until later in the day that I realized I had no headache. I couldn't wait to see the doctor and tell him about it.

"I've had a headache since I was fifteen years old," I said. "Now it's gone. I'm not nervous any more either."

"Good, Very good."

"Will I stay this way?"

"No reason why you shouldn't."

"Doc — what did they do to cure me?"

"You were given electroshock treatments."

"I was that bad?"

"You were pretty bad, Jimmy. The shock treatments got you out of the acute stage. Now you have to do the rest yourself."

"How?" I asked.

"By learning to relax. You must take everything as it comes — in stride. Don't let yourself get upset, no matter how bad things seem. If you feel yourself going off a deep end, stop whatever you're doing, so that you can calm down. You'll have to work at it at first. Later, it will come naturally, just like catching and throwing a baseball."

"That always came naturally to me."

"Only as far as you can remember," the doctor said. "But when you were small, it had to be taught to you. Now you're going to teach yourself how to relax. You can do that, too."

I looked around. We were sitting in one corner of the violent room.

"How can I relax here?"

"We'll get you out tomorrow, and let you have a room to yourself for a little while."

"When can I see my wife?"

"Tomorrow afternoon."

"Doc, how is she?"

"Wonderful," he said. "A fine girl. Until we told her to stop, she came out here every day — and it's a three quarters of an hour drive for her."

"Why did you tell her not to come?"

The doctor shrugged.

"It was just a long trip for nothing. She couldn't see you."

"You say it's a three quarters of an hour drive. From where?"

"From where you live, on Walnut Street in Newton. You rented a house there."

I frowned and rubbed my forehead, as if I were trying to bring some forgotten detail out of it. I didn't remember renting a house in Newton or any other suburb of Boston. *I must have stayed with the Red Sox. But how could that be? They were going to make me into a shortstop.*

"How long did I stay with the Red Sox?" I asked.

"About half the season. They sent you to Birmingham late in June, but not because they weren't satisfied with the way you played."

"Why, then?"

"Well," the doctor said, "you were pretty nervous. They thought that by sending you to a place where you had had such a wonderful season the year before, they could get you to calm down."

"How did I end up here then?"

"I'll tell you in the morning. You've talked enough today."

I was given a room of my own in the morning, and the doctor came in to see me at about eleven o'clock.

"When's Mary coming?" I asked.

"Around two. How do you feel today?"

"Swell. It's great to get out of that — other room."

"I'll bet it is, Jimmy."

"When do I get back into circulation?"

"In a little while — a few weeks ought to do it. You'll stay here for a couple of days, and then we'll put you in with a group of fellows who are convalescing."

"I'm anxious to see Mary."

"And she's anxious to see you," the doctor said. "I just spoke to her a few minutes ago. She and the children send their love, and she can't wait to see you."

The children? There was Eileen — and, yes, I remember — Doreen. That's right — we have two little girls now. Let me see — when was Doreen born? I remember — on March 5 — Eileen's first birthday. Mary called me from Scranton to tell me.

"I have two girls, haven't I, Doc?" I said.

"You remember the birth of the second one?"

"Sure. Mary phoned. I was in Sarasota with the Red Sox, so I couldn't get to Scranton."

"You were there just before Doreen was born."

"I was?"

"Yes. You had a few days off between the end of the special training school and the beginning of regular spring

[123]

training. Jimmy, you remember Doreen's birth. What else do you remember?"

I hesitated, then said, "Well, it's hard to say because everything is so hazy."

"What's the last clear recollection you have, outside of Doreen's birth?"

"Walking into the Terrace at Sarasota, when I reported for that special training school. I remember getting out of the limousine and taking my suitcase and going over the patio and stepping into the lobby and —"

I stopped.

"— and what?" the doctor asked, gently.

"And — nothing. I guess that's all."

I looked hard at the doctor.

"Good Lord," I said, slowly, "that was January 15. Have I been out of my head ever since?"

"I told you, Jimmy — you were a very sick boy. Can you remember anything else?"

"I've got some vague impressions. Seems to me I borrowed Paul Schreiber's glove in Sarasota. He's the Red Sox batting-practice pitcher. I asked him if I could use the glove when he wasn't pitching and he said it was O.K. I think he gave the glove to me later."

"Where was your own glove?"

"I left it home."

"Why?"

"Because the Red Sox were going to make me into a shortstop, and I figured they couldn't do that if I didn't have a glove."

"I see," said the doctor, casually. "Do you remember anything else?"

"Not really. It seems to me I had a terrible argument with an umpire somewhere, but I couldn't tell you exactly where or what it was all about. It must have been after the baseball season began, though, because there was a big crowd."

"What else?"

I thought awhile, then said, "I guess that's all, Doc."

"I see."

"Doc — how come I remember all the details about Doreen's birth, but I can't recall anything else that happened since last January?" I asked.

"Because Doreen's birth was something good — something that you wanted to remember. You see, Jimmy, shock treatments often cause amnesia in some form or other. It can be partial or, as in your case, practically total. This is particularly true about unpleasant events. Almost everything that happened to you while you were sick was unpleasant, and you've forgotten it because you wanted to forget it. But the one pleasant thing that did happen — your little girl's birth — is just as clear in your mind as it would have been if you had been perfectly normal at the time."

The doctor, a pile of newspapers under his arm, dropped in on me after lunch. We talked for a few minutes, then he said, "Here — these papers are for you. Take a look at the sports pages."

We talked for a few minutes, then, after he went out,

I picked up one of the papers. I turned to the sports page, and became absorbed in the first story I had read about the Red Sox since I had been sick. As soon as I finished one paper, I turned to another. The doctor had given me not only eight Boston papers but both the Worcester papers as well.

I was still reading when I heard a step, followed by a rich, soft, marvelously familiar, "Hello, Jimmy, honey —"

I looked up, then jumped to my feet. Mary was standing there, her arms outstretched, her mouth half open, her blue eyes brimming. My own eyes misted and my throat constricted as I walked towards her, and the next thing we knew, we were laughing and crying together in each other's arms.

After a while, she said, "You're all right now."

She was stating a fact, not asking a question.

"I know, honey. I'm O.K. I'll be out of here soon. Tell me about the babies."

She was there for three hours, telling me all the latest news about Eileen and Doreen and Mom and Dad and George and the house and our friends in Scranton and Waterbury, while I just sat and stared at her. When it was time for her to leave, she stood up and the lowering sun, coming in through the window, caught her hair, and it glistened like copper. I grinned and said, "Gee, honey, I guess you *are* a redhead, after all. Remember — that time in the Tiptoe?"

"How can I ever forget the Tiptoe?" she exclaimed.

"Well, the night before Tony introduced us, I asked him who the redhead was."

"I've told you and told you I'm not a redhead. My hair is brown. Don't call me a redhead."

We both laughed. Then I kissed her and asked, "When are you coming back?"

"Tomorrow afternoon. And you know what? Dr. Brown said that after that I can see you twice a day, in the afternoon and in the evening."

"That'll be wonderful, honey. Only — well, he told me it's three quarters of an hour each way. If you make two trips, you'll be riding three hours a day."

"Don't you think it is worth it?"

"It's worth it to me."

"Well, silly," she said, "it's worth it to me, too."

The doctor let me have a radio when I was moved to the convalescent ward. This was a pleasant, sunny room, big enough to accommodate eight men. All of us were in nonviolent stages of our sickness. The doctor assured me that I would be able to go outdoors soon, and it wouldn't be long after that before I would be released from the hospital.

Each day I listened to the broadcast of the Red Sox game. When Mary was with me, we would sit hand in hand, and after it was over she would say, "Next year, honey, you'll be with them," and I'd nod and breathe to myself, "Please, God, let her be right."

Neither she nor the doctor told me any details of what I had been doing on the ball field while I was with the Red Sox, but I knew that I had been acting queerly most of the time.

"When you get back home," the doctor said, "you can

look at the newspaper clippings and see for yourself. Mary can tell you anything you want her to then. Right now I want you to concentrate on getting well."

"What's the matter — are you afraid I'll start worrying about myself?"

He smiled.

"No, I'm not afraid of that. But you've got to think about the future now. You can pick up the past later."

"You know, Doc," I said, soberly, "that's no joke — about my worrying, I mean. I've always been a worrier."

"Sure — and you've always had a headache, too. The headache's gone. So has the worrying. It's all over now. You've been cured. You're starting from scratch. It's as if you had just been born again."

"But if I'm afraid that something will go wrong —"

"It's that fear which you have to avoid. You worried yourself into this place by being afraid of the future. You thought the whole world was against you."

"The Red Sox," I corrected him.

"No, the world."

"But it was after I read that the Red Sox were going to change me from an outfielder to a shortstop that I fell apart."

"If that hadn't made you do it, something else would have. You were ripe for a crackup, that's all. And the reason you were ripe was your fear of the unknown. That's been knocked out of you now. You must keep it out."

It was Mary who first told me that I had started the 1952 season at shortstop for the Red Sox.

"I *started* the season?" I said, incredulously.

"You were a darn good shortstop," she told me.

"But I thought Boudreau had said if I looked promising he'd send me to the minors for a year."

"He did say it, and I suppose he intended to do it, but you were better than he expected you to be, so he kept you. If you hadn't been so nervous and upset, he'd probably have left you at shortstop right along."

"But I'm not a shortstop."

"You were for a while," she said. "You had the job for the first month of the season — and you did well at it, too."

Now it was early September, and I was permitted to go outside and play ball in the warm sun. Mary was allowed to tell me more about myself, while Dr. Brown was preparing me for my release from the hospital.

"How bad was I — with Boudreau, I mean?" I asked Mary, one day.

"Pretty bad, honey. You were so terribly nervous that he wasn't sure what to do with you. Neither was anyone else, for that matter."

"But what did I do?" I persisted.

"I'll show you when we go through the scrapbooks at home. Anyhow, Boudreau benched you after a month, and then he shifted you back to the outfield."

"And that didn't straighten me out?"

"By then, I guess nothing could have straightened you

out," she said. "You acted more and more peculiar, so they finally sent you to Birmingham."

"So the doctor told me. I don't remember going to Birmingham at all."

"Well," she said, wryly, "they remember you all right."

"Was I very bad there, too?"

She nodded.

"You came back to Boston twice," she said. "The second time — you stayed."

"Here?"

"No. First they took you to a private sanitarium, but you got violent, so they had you transferred to the State Hospital at Danvers. That's over on the North Shore, out of the district where we live, so they shifted you here to Westborough."

"I'm glad they did. Otherwise, I'd never have run into Dr. Brown."

"He's a swell guy, all right," Mary said. "He told me over and over that you were going to recover, and that was the only thing that kept me going."

One day Dr. Brown handed me a fistful of letters and cards.

"These are for you," he said. "Read them."

"For me? Who'd write me here?"

"Friends — and fans."

I picked one up and looked at the signature, but it meant nothing to me. The letter, written in a schoolboy scrawl, was short and sweet. It read:

"DEAR JIMMY, I watched you play all the time you were with the Red Sox and for my money you're the best

[130]

outfielder in baseball. Please get well so that I'll be able to watch you again next year."

I laid it aside and looked at a postcard. That one said, "Stay with it, Jimmy. We're all pulling for you."

The other letters and cards were written along the same lines. As I read them one by one, my eyes smarted and I couldn't swallow. When I looked up at the doctor, the tears began to flow, and without shame, I let them come. After a while, I pulled myself together and said, "These people are strangers, yet look at the trouble they go to for me."

"They're not strangers, Jimmy," he said, softly. "They're fans — and fans are friends. They want you to know they're with you, that's all."

Every day after that, I was given new mail to read. Sometimes Dr. Brown would bring it in, sometimes an attendant would pass it along, sometimes Mary would have a batch of it with her. The letters had always been opened before I saw them, and obviously had been screened.

"Who's the censor?" I asked Mary.

She laughed.

"Two of us," she said. "The doctor and me."

"Do I see everything?"

"Everything good."

"Is there much — bad?" I asked.

"Very little. You see practically everything."

One day, an attendant gave me several letters, and as I looked through them, I noticed that one was sealed. I tore it open and a clipping from a New Orleans newspaper fell out. New Orleans has a team in the Southern Association, and I had played there often when I was with Birmingham.

The clipping was a copy of a column of notes written by a sports writer. One line was circled in red pencil and my eyes widened in fright when I read it. It said, "Jimmy Piersall, former Barons outfielder, who practically tore the ball park apart with his mad antics the last time he was here, will never play baseball again. Now a hopeless mental case, he will spend the rest of his life in an institution right outside of Boston."

I sank down on my bed, my head in my hands, and closed my eyes. *What is this? Have the doc and Mary and everyone else been kidding me? They talk about my leaving here soon and give me letters of encouragement and tell me how well I'm getting along. Is this all an act? What's going on? I've got to know. I'll see the doc right now.* I felt a hand on my shoulders.

"What's the matter, Jimmy?"

Dr. Brown was standing beside me. I looked up, shrugged in a gesture of despair, then silently handed him the clipping. He read it quickly. I watched his face closely. He started to frown, but then his mouth relaxed in a smile.

"This guy must have better information about you than I have," he said, lightly.

"You mean what he says isn't true?"

The doc sat down beside me.

"Of course it's not true, Jimmy. What ever in the world gave you the idea it was?"

"You mean I really am getting along fine and I really will leave here soon and I really can play ball again? You and Mary and everyone else have been leveling with me, not kidding? Is that what you mean?"

"Certainly that's what I mean," the doctor said. "Look, Jimmy, how could a New Orleans sports writer know anything about what's going on with a patient in a hospital nearly two thousand miles away?"

"Well, how could a man write a thing like this then? He wouldn't do it unless he had some basis in fact, would he?"

"Jimmy, I don't know anything about this writer, but I know a lot about you — a great deal more than he does. You're practically well. Pretty soon, you'll be able to go home. By next season, you'll be back with the Red Sox. Can I make it any plainer?"

The doctor was looking squarely into my eyes. *This man must mean what he's saying. He can't be that good an actor. That New Orleans sports columnist has to be wrong. Come to think of it, anyone who hasn't seen me lately and writes a thing like that has to be wrong.* I leaned back, resting my elbows on the bed, and breathed a long sigh.

"I guess you can't," I said. "But how can a guy write such things?"

"He's got to fill up his column with something. Does it all have to be true?"

"Well, there are guys like that, although most of the writers I've met have been swell."

Then I looked at the doctor and grinned, slyly.

[133]

"You'd better get your censors back on the job," I said. "The one they let get away was certainly a beauty."

One Sunday, Mary walked in and said, "You've got company outside."

"Who?"

"Ed Foley."

"Who?" I said again.

"Ed Foley — oh, gosh, honey — you don't remember ever having met him, do you?"

"No, I don't."

"He lives next door. He's your best friend in Boston."

"What do I say to the guy?"

"Let's ask Dr. Brown."

We met him in one of the corridors.

"What do I do when I meet my best friend and don't recognize him?" I asked.

"Just what you'd do when you meet any good friend. Greet him warmly, shake hands with him and say whatever you feel like saying."

Ed Foley turned out to be a tall, friendly dark-haired man, a member of the Newton police force. He walked towards me with his hand outstretched, and I met him halfway. I let him lead the conversation and, after a while, I began to feel right at home with him. By the time he was ready to leave, I felt that we were good friends again. But I sought out the doctor the minute he was gone.

"It was all right this time," I said, "because Ed came with Mary and she told me that he was here. But what shall I do if I don't get any warning in advance? I won't recognize a guy and he'll think I'm high-hatting him."

"Don't let it worry you. Any time you're greeted with warmth and enthusiasm by someone who claims to be an old friend, tell him the truth. Say that you can't remember anything that happened during the period that you were sick, and that you're sorry, but you don't recognize him."

"Won't he think it's funny?"

"Why should he? If he's really a good friend, he'll understand."

Early one afternoon, the doctor asked me if I'd like to see my dad. During the first few weeks of my convalescence, I had been reluctant to talk to him. I can't tell you why. I only know that I wasn't ready to face him until I was more sure of myself. The very fact that Dr. Brown mentioned the idea of seeing my father at all was a good thing. He knew that I loved my dad, but he hadn't wanted me exposed to any of the old fears. *He thinks I can take it now. And I know I can take it.*

"I want to see Dad," I said. "It's been pretty rough for him — not being able to come near me all this time."

"Good," said the doctor. "He's waiting for you on the grounds now. Your mother and the Tracys are with him."

I kissed Mom and shook hands all around, and it felt good to see them all. They had brought a picnic lunch, and we sat outside and ate it. Everyone treated me casually, but I caught Mom looking sharply at me a few times.

She looks at me and she looks around this place and I know exactly what she's thinking. She's remembering

those days at Norwich and they're not pleasant memories.
And she's wondering how long it's going to be with me.

I walked over and put my arm around her waist and said, lightly, "I'll be out of here in a couple of weeks, and the doctor says I'll never be back."

She smiled at me, and I hope it made her feel better. *Poor Mom. Life wasn't too good to her in her younger days. But it's going to be all right from now on.*

The following Sunday, right after Mary left, a car drove up to the front entrance just as I was getting ready to go inside, and two couples stepped out. I looked at them casually, then looked again. The party consisted of Ellis Kinder, the veteran Red Sox pitcher, and his wife Ruth, Ted Lepcio, then a rookie Red Sox infielder, and Mary Trank, who worked in the Red Sox ticket office. Kinder had always been nice to me when I was with the club in the latter part of the 1950 season, and during spring training in 1951. Everyone liked Mary, who used to take her vacation at Sarasota in the spring. I recognized Lepcio from his pictures. I didn't remember ever having met him. *Nice of him to come — but why should he be particularly interested in me?* He was a Seton Hall College graduate who had had only one year in professional baseball before joining the Red Sox in the spring of 1952. He started the 1951 season at Roanoke, Virginia, in the Class B Piedmont League while I was with the Red Sox, and finished it at Louisville while I was at Birmingham, so, as far as I knew, our paths had never crossed.

But he acted as if he knew me well, and I greeted him warmly. *He must have been close to me while I was sick.*

[136]

I'll ask Mary. I was glad to see them all, because, aside from a visit from Joe Cronin, the Red Sox general manager, this was the only time any Red Sox people had been to see me. We talked baseball for an hour or so, and I was pleased to see that all four acted perfectly natural with me. I was sorry when the time came for them to leave, but they all assured me that they'd see me again soon.

"You'll be out of here before the end of the season," Kinder said. "Then you can get over to the ball park."

"If you can't," added Lepcio, "we'll surely see you in Sarasota next spring."

I asked Mary about Lepcio the next day.

"He was the best friend you had on the ball club," she told me. "He stood up for you and protected you and kept telling everyone you were all right and did everything he could to help you."

Then she explained that Lepcio had been my roommate, not only during spring training in Sarasota, but all during the time that I was with the Red Sox. Whenever I got into arguments, which was often, he used to push me away and take over, particularly when it appeared as though I might be exposing myself to a punch in the nose. He was ready to fight for me whenever anyone showed intense resentment at my bitter wisecracks and belligerent outlook. He encouraged me when I was low and was the first to pat me on the back when I did well. Of all the guys on the ball club, he was the last to give up on me. The others, disgusted, maybe a little scared, upset and weary of my antics on the field and raucous bragging off it, eventually ignored me. Lepcio stuck with me until the last minute. When I was sent to Birmingham in June of 1952 he was the only man on the club speaking to me.

"Holy cow," I said to Mary, "if I hadn't seen pictures of him, I wouldn't have known what he looked like."

"Well, honey, he was a real friend."

"Were there many others?"

"Quite a few," she said. "You'll meet them as we go along."

The doctor told me not to worry about it.

"A lot of things will come up from time to time," he explained. "Just take them in stride. Don't be surprised at anything that happens."

"When do I get out of here?"

"Soon — very soon. Sooner than you think."

I was released from Westborough on September 9, 1952, almost six weeks to the day after I went in. The doctor told me the night before.

"You're going home tomorrow, Jimmy," he said. "As far as we're concerned, you're cured."

"That's wonderful, Doc. Thanks a million for all you did for me."

"I haven't done a thing. You did it all yourself. Now, when you get home, take it very slowly for a while. Don't get excited or upset about anything. When you meet anyone, be casual and talk as if the last time you saw him was yesterday. Take light exercise at first — you know, like what you were doing playing around the grounds here. After a while, you can do more, but don't try to lick the world right off. And I wouldn't drive a car for a while."

"How long?"

"Oh, five or six weeks. And when you do drive, don't try to break any speed records or beat the other fellow to the punch. If someone wants to pass you or tries to cut you out, let him. If he honks his horn at you, laugh at him. People who drive that way don't have any sense. I ought to know. I do it myself. But don't you."

"I'm a little scared, Doc," I said. "Suppose something comes up that I can't handle?"

"Nothing will. You can cope with anything. Remember that. You're no different from anyone else now, and your problems won't be any different from other people's. Just don't try to manufacture new ones, and you'll be all right."

"Aren't people likely to sort of steer clear of me?"

"Some will. Most won't. You'll find that the world is full of people who want to help you."

"I've found that out already."

"It'll be the same wherever you go," he said.

"What if people make cracks like that New Orleans writer did? Or ask me about — this place?"

"Don't get upset. That's the main thing. Just laugh off things like that. If anyone asks you about Westborough, tell them it's a country club or something. Don't worry about it."

"I'll try not to," I said. Then — "Doc, I wonder how many people will be staring at me and saying to themselves, 'He's been away once. He'll probably go back some day'?"

"What do you care? You don't have to worry about what people think. And, if they think that, you'll know they're wrong. You've been sick. Now you're well again. It's as simple as that. Most people will understand. The few who don't won't bother you unless you let them. Remember, Jimmy — you're well and you'll stay well as long as you want to stay well. Your mental health is in nobody's hands but your own now. You can control it. Mary will help you. She's a very wonderful girl, you know. And if by some chance you feel you need more help than she can give you, I'll be no farther away from you than the nearest telephone. Call me whenever you want to."

"And how about all those crazy things I was supposed to have done while I was playing ball this year? Is it all right for Mary to tell me all about them now?"

"Perfectly O.K. I think you should know about those things. She tells me your father kept a scrapbook of newspaper clippings. Have him bring it to you, and go over it with Mary."

"And how about the details of when I actually cracked up? I want to know them too."

"I think you should know," the doctor said. "Let Mary tell you."

"Does she know the whole story?"

"Know it? Believe me, Jimmy, there's nobody in this whole wide world who knows it better. She lived it."

Mary and Ed came for me the next day, and as I walked out of the place for the last time, I silently repeated a fervent prayer of thanks to God for the help He had given me. The doctor, his brown eyes bright, his step jaunty, his dark face wreathed in a wide smile, walked down to the car with us. When he shook hands, he said, "I'm glad you're leaving, Jimmy, but I'll miss you."

"I'll miss you, too, Doc. I wouldn't have made it without you."

"Good luck. I'll go to Fenway Park and watch you play ball for the Red Sox next spring."

"Look for me in the outfield," I said, with a grin. "You won't find me at shortstop."

Dad brought his scrapbooks up from Waterbury a few days after I got home. Feeling a little like a man about to attend his own funeral, I opened the one marked "1952," and slowly began going through it. It took me a couple of weeks of reading and talking things over with Mary, but I insisted on seeing everything. I wanted to piece it all together in chronological order. It was my life. This dreadful stage of it was an open book to thousands of baseball fans all over the country. I couldn't let it remain closed to me.

To my utter amazement, I discovered that I acted quite normal in Sarasota. My blackout when I first stepped into the hotel lobby was complete but entirely internal. Outwardly I showed no more than signs of routine rookie nervousness. When I recalled how I felt that morning after getting out of the airport limousine, it seemed to me that I must have staggered across the lobby, or even passed out cold on the way to the desk, but nothing like that happened. I walked over to register without even breaking my stride. I checked in, let a bellhop pick up my grip, went up in the elevator and was met in my room by Lepcio, who got in ahead of me.

The Red Sox made it plain the first week of the special training school that they were grooming Ted and me to be the new second-base combination. "Lepcio is the Red Sox second baseman of the future," one story read, "and Piersall is the shortstop of the future. Both look very promising, and in another year or so, they might have their jobs sewed up for many years to come."

Since Lepcio was only a few months younger than I, close observers of the club figured that we'd be established stars for a long time. Ted was twenty-one at the time; I was twenty-two.

"I was really a good shortstop then?" I asked Mary.

"I should say you were. If you don't believe me, look at the clippings. They can tell you more about how you were doing on the field than I can. After all, the men who wrote those stories were right on the spot. I was still in Scranton waiting to have Doreen."

I flipped the pages of the scrapbook, and then came to a clipping that seemed unbelievable.

"Jim Piersall is a big-league shortstop already," it read. "He's been given intensive instruction by two of the greatest shortstops of modern times, and they're both satisfied with him."

"Cronin and Boudreau," I remarked to Mary. "And they both thought I was good?"

"Good enough to start the season at shortstop for the Red Sox."

"This I've got to see."

"Well, look at the box score on opening day," she said.

I flipped the pages of the scrapbook until I came to the morning-newspaper clippings of April 16, 1952, which carried reports of ball games the day before. The Red Sox opened in Washington that year, and the first thing that caught my eye was a picture of President Truman throwing out the first ball.

"The President saw me play shortstop," I said, hardly believing.

"So did a few thousand other people," Mary commented.

I ran my eye down the Red Sox batting order — DiMaggio, center field; Pesky, third base; Williams, left field; Dropo, first base; Thronsberry, right field; *Piersall, shortstop* —

The Red Sox won a 3–0 victory over Washington that day, and I played a good, if unspectacular, game. I got one hit — a ground-rule double that bounced into the center-field bull pen — took part in a double play and made no errors.

In the *Boston Daily Record,* Joe Cashman, who covered the game, wrote: "Piersall hit the longest drive of the game and handled everything that came his way at short, a position he was playing for the first time in a championship contest."

I looked at Mary and said, "Honey, I made the ball club at shortstop the first year they tried me there, and I'd never played the position before in my life. Shouldn'7 that have convinced me that the Red Sox really wanted me?"

"It should have, I suppose, but I guess it was too late then."

"I know — but how did I act towards you and towards the children?"

"You were all right, Jimmy, but terribly nervous and I was scared and worried. You were so restless that you couldn't stay still a minute. After the club came to Boston, people started asking you to go out and speak at smokers and dinners and all sorts of men's groups."

Speak in public? I'd never done any public speaking in my life before. What did I do? What did I say?

"Mary —"

"Yes, honey."

"I must have made a terrible fool of myself."

"What do you mean?"

"I mean — when I went out to speak in public. I wonder what stupid things I might have said."

"Well, I never heard you, but people who did say you were great. After a few weeks, you were in such big demand that you had to turn down invitations to go out. But by then the real storm signals had started."

"How?"

"An umpire threw you out of a ball game at the Yankee Stadium in New York," she said. "That was the first bad thing that happened in public. Here — look at the clippings. It was early in May, I think."

I turned more pages and finally came to a report of the game between the Red Sox and the Yankees on May

11. Piersall was still playing shortstop. Early in the game, Gil McDougald of the Yankees hit a ground ball to him which he fielded and threw to Billy Goodman, who was playing first base for the Red Sox. The throw wasn't accurate, and it pulled Goodman off the bag, but he tagged McDougald going by — or at least it looked to Piersall as if he tagged him. Anyhow, Jim Honochick, the umpire, called McDougald safe, and that started Piersall off.

Piersall rushed across the infield and practically swarmed over Honochick, screaming and yelling at the top of his voice that Honochick had missed the play, and every time Honochick turned in another direction, Piersall turned with him, jabbering and howling in his face. Such a performance on the part of a veteran ballplayer is bad enough, and an umpire will nearly always throw a man out of a game for that sort of thing. In a rookie, it was unpardonable. Honochick thumbed Piersall out of there almost at the minute he started protesting and his continued yelling earned him a fine on top of the expulsion.

In the meantime, Goodman, who was right on top of the play and knew better than anyone whether or not he had tagged McDougald, started out by making only a routine perfunctory protest. This is common procedure whenever a play is close, and umpires expect it. A player mutters a mild disagreement with the decision, knowing that the umpire will pay no attention to it.

But when Piersall charged across the diamond, Goodman began yelling at Honochick, and then Boudreau and the coaches came out from the Red Sox dugout behind third base. The argument got hotter and hotter, and it ended up with the Red Sox lodging an official protest — which was disallowed by the league later — after the Yankees won the game — and all on account of that one play.

"Well," I commented to Mary, "that doesn't look so bad to me. Every player, even if he's a rookie, is entitled to one serious squawk a year. And it couldn't have been too unreasonable. Everyone else joined me in yelling at Honochick, and we even protested the game. What was so wrong about that?"

"Nothing, on the surface," said Mary, "but I didn't remember your ever making such a wild scene that the umpire would throw you out."

"I guess that's right. I'd never been thrown out of a game before. I'd never got that mad at an umpire."

"And that's what worried me. I was afraid it might only be the beginning. You were so jittery that it looked as if anything might happen."

"What came next?" I asked her.

"I think the fist fights."

"Fist fights? I never was mixed up in a fight that I can remember — at least not on the ball field."

"Well, honey, you had two in one day — and they came even before the game started."

We found some of the details in the scrapbook. It was two weeks after I had been thrown out of the Stadium game, and we were playing the Yankees again, this time in Boston. During infield practice, I was working at short-stop, and some of the Yankees, including Billy Martin, their young second baseman, were tossing the ball back and forth on the sidelines in front of their dugout behind third base. Martin and I began exchanging insults, cupping our mouths with our hands so we could hear each other. One word led to another, and after a while Martin pointed towards the runway leading to the dressing rooms and began walking towards it.

At that time, the Red Sox and the visitors' locker rooms were side by side at the end of a runway leading in from the Red Sox dugout, which, at Fenway Park, is on the first-base side of the field, so there was nothing unusual about two players from opposing teams heading for the same exit. Today, the Fenway Park visitors use a new locker room under the third-base side of the grandstand, with a separate entrance from their own dugout.

Martin arrived at the runway first, and was waiting for me when I got there. We started swinging on each other, and had exchanged a couple of punches before the fight was broken up by two coaches, Oscar Mellilo of the Red Sox and Bill Dickey of the Yankees. Ellis Kinder, who was pitching for us that day, happened to come by right after the fight started, and he helped pull us apart.

It was all over in a few minutes, and Boudreau told me to go into the locker room and change my shirt. When I got there, Maurice McDermott, one of our pitchers, whose locker was near mine, made some remark, and I took a swing at him. We punched each other a couple of times before that one was broken up, and then Boudreau decided to make me sit the game out.

I guess I put on quite a performance in the dugout that

day. I couldn't stand the idleness, and I prowled back and forth on the bench, cupping my hands and yelling towards the field, hanging by one hand from the dugout roof and swinging myself back and forth like a monkey, moving around from bench to dugout steps and back to bench and changing seats constantly. The guys on the team kept yelling at me to sit still and shut up, but I paid no attention. And whenever Martin came to bat, I crouched on the top step of the dugout and screamed invective at him.

Mary pointed to a picture, showing me yelling at Martin from the dugout, and I said, "What in the world ever happened to start this thing in the first place?"

"I don't know," she replied. "All I know is that there were stories that you and Martin disliked each other on sight and had begun this feud during spring training in Florida."

"I've met Martin and played against him a couple of times before, but I don't remember ever having feuded with him. Honey, how can I ever face a guy like that again? How can I face McDermott? Imagine getting into a locker-room fight with one of your own teammates!"

"I asked you about it when you got home that night, but you told me to mind my own business."

"I did?"

"You told me that often during those days, Jimmy."

I brushed a hand across her cheek and said, "Poor Mary — you took a pretty good beating yourself, didn't you?"

I turned back to the clippings. Right after the game

with the Yankees, Boudreau called McDermott and me into his office off the locker room and made us shake hands. Then, according to one story, he announced, "There will be no more fights among our own players," and, as far as I could tell by the clippings, nothing unusual relating to me happened for several more days. But when I commented on that, Mary said, "No, honey, that's wrong. Everything wasn't in the papers."

"Like what?" I asked.

"Like your imitating DiMaggio's running stride."

"My what?"

She nodded. "That's right," she said. "Boudreau decided to put you back in the outfield, since this shortstop experiment seemed to make you so nervous, and you started to mock the things that DiMaggio did during pregame fielding practice."

DiMaggio had an unusual stride. He ran flat-footed, his legs almost rigid from the knees down, and he flapped his arms like wings with every step. At first, when I was practicing in the outfield, I just imitated him as we came in to the bench, but later, when Boudreau put me in right field beside DiMaggio, who played center, I used to follow him in that way after every inning. I'd fall into step a few feet behind him and run just like him, while the fans in the stands roared. I guess it must have looked pretty funny to them, but it wasn't funny to me when Mary told me about it.

"Dominic DiMaggio was one of my idols, honey," I said. "Why, as long as I can remember, I've wanted to play in the same outfield with him and Williams. But

[149]

when I got the chance to play next to him, I went out of my way to make him look silly."

"You were sick," she said. "You didn't know what you were doing. DiMaggio will understand the situation. All the ballplayers will understand it."

"What else did I do that I won't read about in the clippings?"

"Well, you drove Boudreau crazy trying to get him to put you back into the lineup."

Boudreau, after deciding to shift me back to the outfield, kept me on the bench for several days. Neither he nor the players could quiet me down, but he sometimes got me to sit still by moving in beside me and talking to me. He kept telling me that he expected to put me into right field as soon as I had calmed down, and he advised me to get used to the position. I had always been a center fielder, but right field at Fenway Park is very hard to play. It's not only the sun field, but the grandstand turns sharply in one corner, with the result that the ball bounces peculiarly when it hits the wall. Some of the caroms it can take are almost unpredictable.

Even so, Boudreau had no doubts about my ability to play the position. At that point, he wasn't even concerned too much about my hitting. All he wanted to do was tone me down enough so that I could play ball without driving everyone around me to distraction. The only trouble was that the longer I sat on the bench, the more nervous I became.

As a result, not a day or a night went by without my hounding Boudreau to put me back in the lineup. I'd get to the ball park early and see him in his office before most of the other players were there. After he posted the day's lineup on the bulletin board in the locker room, I'd go after him again. Then, just before the game started, I'd try to get him to change his mind, and even if I got in for a few innings, I'd rush back to his office after the game and say, "How about tomorrow, Lou? Am I going to be in?"

He was using Clyde Vollmer in right field during this period. Vollmer was a powerful veteran, known among baseball men as a streak hitter. When Vollmer was hot, no pitcher in the world could fool him for very long. He'd get two and three hits a game for a week at a time, and if we were at Fenway Park, he'd sock home runs in clusters, since he was a right-handed pull hitter. He once won eight or ten ball games in less than three weeks with key hits, and from that time on he became known as Dutch the Clutch.

"When Vollmer is hot," Boudreau used to say, "I wouldn't put Ty Cobb or Babe Ruth in his place. And you never know when the guy might get hot."

But when Vollmer was cold, he was just another journeyman ballplayer. A big, somewhat clumsy man, he was not fast enough to be a top-notch outfielder. He could be used effectively only when he was in a hitting streak.

When Vollmer started cooling off at the plate, Boudreau put me in his place during the later part of ball games, mostly for defensive purposes. That set me off on a new series of stunts which attracted so much attention that I became a national baseball figure almost overnight.

When I got into a game late, I was able to make a flamboyant entrance, and I took full advantage of the opportunity.

The right fielder at Fenway Park has thousands of fans sitting within hailing distance, both in the corner of the grandstand which extends all along the foul line and in the right-field section of the bleachers. The fans began calling for me about the fifth or sixth inning, and the ball park would ring with the chant, "We want Piersall! We want Piersall!" At first, I simply exchanged a few wisecracks when I ran out to the position to replace Vollmer, but I developed new bits of business every day, and pretty soon I had a ritual to which the fans responded wholeheartedly.

When I first ran out to my position, I took off my hat and waved it, bowing in all directions. Then, I began a complicated set of mock calisthenics, which took several minutes. After that, I started playing catch with someone in the Red Sox bull pen, which was in right center field. This game lasted only a short time, because the boys in the bull-pen crew were most reluctant to co-operate. Besides, the umpires were always after me to settle down so the ball game could be resumed.

In the meantime, the fans were roaring and cheering and clapping their hands, and every gesture of encouragement goaded me on to new heights of clowning. When I caught a ball, I bowed with elaborate exaggeration, no matter how easy the chance. If I made a sensational catch, I shrugged it off as routine. After a while I couldn't make a move without drawing laughter and applause from the stands.

When the inning was over, I always let DiMaggio get ahead of me, and then went through that routine of shadowing him with his own step, and I guess that brought the house down. In those days it was customary for fielders to leave their gloves at their positions instead of taking them into the dugout when going in to bat. According to today's rules, fielders take their gloves with them after each inning.

When we'd go back to take our positions, the fans got into the habit of maintaining a dead silence as I ran out. Then, when I picked up my glove, they burst into a tremendous cheer, and I waved my hat, then clasped my hands together like a boxer before going through the calisthenics act.

"I must have killed them," I said, soberly, to Mary. "What are those fans going to do to me, do you suppose?"

"They're not going to hurt you," she said. "No matter what caused you to do those things, the fans enjoyed watching you."

"Do you suppose they'll expect me to do all that stuff again, honey? Because I never did it before, and I could never do it again."

"All the fans want to do is help you. That's all anyone wants to do. They won't expect you to do anything that will be harmful to you."

I turned the pages of the scrapbook. I was starting a game here and there, because Vollmer's hitting streak was over, but Boudreau was also using Faye Thronsberry, a rookie, and Ken Wood, a veteran, in right field. I was showing no signs of settling down, and Boudreau, confused and upset himself over the situation, didn't know whether to play me or not. If he played me, I went through my act and distracted everybody in the ball park. If he didn't I hounded him to death. One course of action seemed just as bad as the other.

One afternoon in early June, the Red Sox pulled a big trade with Detroit. We sent Walt Dropo, Fred Hatfield, Johnny Pesky, Bill Wight and Don Lenhardt to the Tigers for George Kell, Johnny Lipon, Dizzy Trout and Hoot Evers. Dropo was a first baseman. Pesky and Lipon were shortstops who could also play second base. Hatfield was a third baseman, Lenhardt and Evers were outfielders and Wight and Trout were pitchers. Kell, the best third baseman in the American League at the time, was the key man in the trade.

We had a night game in Boston against the Cleveland Indians on that date, while the Tigers were playing the Athletics in Philadelphia. As soon as the trade was announced, the five men leaving our club flew out to join the Tigers. The four former Detroit players coming to us were due in town in time for our game that night.

But they were delayed, and none of them had arrived when Boudreau posted the lineups in the locker room. It looked as if we were going to be short of infielders. According to Mary, Boudreau called me into his office and said, "Jimmy, I'm putting you down to play shortstop tonight. Now just go out there and take it easy. Don't try to be funny. Just concentrate on getting ready for the game. And remember — this is only a provisional lineup. If Lipon shows up in time, he'll be our shortstop."

I galloped out to the field and worked around shortstop like a man possessed. I cut in front of other guys to take balls during infield practice. I jumped around getting throws meant for somebody else, I ran back and forth between second base and third, yelling encouragement and instructions to everyone within hearing, and I generally made a pest of myself. But I was happy, because I was back in action, and I was sure everything would be fine when Boudreau told me to take batting practice with the regulars.

But half an hour before the game, when I walked into the dugout, Boudreau pulled me aside and said, "The others just arrived. I'm sorry, Jimmy, but Lipon's going to play short tonight."

I went off in a corner of the dugout, broke down and cried. I wept for ten or fifteen minutes, right out there where everyone who went near the dugout could see me. The next day the sports pages carried the story of my sobbing breakdown. It was right there, in print, for all the world to see. I blushed to my ears as I read it in the scrapbook.

A few days after the weeping incident, Boudreau decided to give me a real chance to make the club as the right fielder. He announced that I would play there regularly, and I was greeted by my constituents out there like a long-lost brother. After bowing and waving and tipping my cap in response to the reception, I stepped up close to the bleachers, and led the fans in a prolonged and organized cheer for myself. They loved it.

I looked up at Mary and mused, "Y'know, honey, bad as this all looks, I'll have to admit I was a pretty funny guy, at that."

"I should say you were a pretty funny guy. The fans thought you were a real comedian."

"I guess they were right. But where do you suppose I got my ideas from? I never was much of a gagster before. I must have had a suppressed desire to be a clown or something."

"You must have, honey. All I know is I didn't dare pick up the papers every day. I never knew what I was going to read next about you."

I saw what she meant, for the next headline I came across in the scrapbook read, "Rookie Piersall Teases Old Satch Paige."

The story was a graphic description of a game against the St. Louis Browns (now the Baltimore Orioles) the night before at Fenway Park. It had been a real thriller, for the Red Sox scored six runs in the ninth inning to come from far behind to win. Going into that inning, the Browns were ahead, 9–5, and Satchel Paige had gone in to protect their lead.

Paige was a tall, skinny, ageless Negro who, in spite of the fact that he must have been close to fifty then, was one of the best relief pitchers in baseball. Old Satch had every pitching trick in the book and he invented a lot more of his own. When he had his stuff, he was almost impossible to hit, although because of his age he couldn't be used for more than a few innings at a time. He had already pitched two innings that night, but there didn't seem to be any doubt that he'd be able to hold a four-run lead. The fans were beginning to file out of the park when we went up to bat for the last time.

Piersall was the leadoff man, and he wasn't figured to have much chance to do anything with the old guy. But, according to the stories, Piersall cupped his hands and yelled, "I'm gonna bunt, Satch!" He not only bunted the first pitch, but beat it out for a hit, and then, as a base runner, he began driving Paige crazy with a new set of zany antics.

When Paige wound up to pitch, he looked like a cross between Ichabod Crane and Rip Van Winkle. Instead of giving his arms full play, as most hurlers do, so they can put all their strength into a pitch, Paige, his bony elbow sticking out at right angles to his body, only brought his long right arm up halfway, and he did it in slow motion. Then he brought his hands down in front of him and fired the ball. He was easy to imitate and funny to watch, unless you were the batter trying to hit against him.

Hoot Evers was up for the Red Sox, but the fans were watching Piersall. As he led off from first base, he began putting on a vaudeville act that convulsed the customers and had Paige mumbling to himself. Every move Paige made Piersall made. Every time Paige turned towards first base, Piersall mirrored the turn as he skipped back to the bag. When Paige stood still and looked towards the plate, Piersall flapped his arms like a chicken and made noises like a pig. The fans were yelling and laughing and clap-

[157]

ping their hands, but all the harassed Paige could hear was Piersall's "Oink! Oink! Oink!" from first base.

Paige finally managed to start pitching to Evers, who eventually got an infield hit that moved Piersall to second base. George Kell was the next hitter. Piersall danced and howled and mugged and imitated and flapped and oinked from second base now, and Paige was trying very hard not to pay any attention. In the meantime, the cagy Kell ran the count to three balls and two strikes, then fouled off a succession of Paige's best pitches. The old man was beginning to feel his age, perhaps, because he finally threw a fourth ball at Kell and that filled the bases with nobody out.

Now on third base, Piersall cupped his hands and oinked and kept repeating, "You're the funniest sight I ever saw, Satchmo," and aped his motion and whistled and screamed, while Paige went to work on Vern Stephens, the next hitter. Stephens popped out, and that brought up Billy Goodman with the bases still full, one out and the Red Sox still trailing, 9–5.

But Paige had lost control of the situation. He walked Goodman on five pitches, forcing Piersall home with the sixth run. As Piersall trotted between third base and the plate, he laughed and screamed and imitated Paige some more, and Satch tried to ignore him, but was really upset by then. Ted Lepcio followed Goodman by hitting a clean single to drive Evers home, and that cut the Browns' lead to 9–7. The bases were still full, and Sammy White, the Red Sox catcher, was up.

By this time, the stands were in an uproar. Piersall was

crouching on the top step of the dugout, his hands cupped over his mouth, and the oinks were pouring out as fast as he could say them. White was a right-handed hitter with a lot of power. Old Satch kept his back to the Red Sox dugout so he couldn't see Piersall, but he knew Piersall was still yelling at him.

He turned and tried to concentrate on White, and for a while it looked as if Satch might get him. The count went to two strikes and one ball, but then Paige threw one pitch too many. Sammy whipped his bat around and the ball sailed over that short left field-fence for a grand-slam home run. White was so happy that he did a little clowning himself. As he came home from third base, he got down on his hands and knees, then crawled the last ten feet and kissed the plate.

White's homer won the game, of course, but Piersall got most of the publicity. John Drohan, veteran *Boston Traveler* baseball writer, put it this way:

"Jim Piersall, who threatens to become the greatest baseball attraction the Red Sox ever had — if he doesn't get killed by a pitched ball — took last night's spotlight away from the game's pitching attraction for three decades, Pitcher Satchel Paige.

"Even though Sammy White hit the grand-slam homer that beat the Browns 11–9 in one of the greatest Donnybrooks ever seen in Fenway Park, Sam pointed to the laughing Piersall and said, 'There's the guy who made it possible.' "

The reference to the danger of my being killed by a pitched ball, while facetious, did contain a grain of sobriety. Both pitchers and umpires had developed an intense — and understandable — dislike for me. From what I was told and from what I read in the scrapbook, I spent a lot of time on my back, hitting the dirt to get out of the way of pitches that might otherwise have crowned me.

Ever since the Yankee Stadium incident with Honochick, my relations with umpires (and theirs with me) had been very shaky indeed. They cracked down on me whenever they could find an excuse, and I gave them plenty. Before I was through, I paid so many fines to Will Harridge, the president of the American League, that I finally sent him a note reading, "If this keeps up, I'll be paying some umpire's salary."

One day, while I stood at the plate, clowning and mocking every move made by Connie Marrero, veteran Washington Senators pitcher, he threw three straight strikes at me. I just watched them go by without taking my bat off my shoulder. Then, when Art Passarella, who was umpiring the plate, called me out, I whirled and yelled, "I wouldn't want to have that on my conscience!"

Two days after the Satchel Paige game in Boston, the Red Sox started on a Western trip. Since our home stand had been a long one, most of my clowning had been at Fenway Park.

Now the fans around the country, who had been hearing about Piersall through their local newspapers, were looking forward to watching him perform in the flesh.

Chicago was the first stop. Comiskey Park, where the White Sox play, is almost surrounded by a high double-decked grandstand, so the fans and the right fielder are, as at Fenway Park, within easy hailing distance of each other. Piersall spent his first day there getting acquainted. He exchanged wisecracks, did some calisthenics, took a few bows, and generally gave the customers a taste of what to expect from him.

There was a Sunday doubleheader the next day, and over forty thousand people, one of the biggest White Sox crowds of the year, came out to watch it. Piersall must have been inspired by the mob — or maybe it was inspired by him — and he put on one of the corniest and most confusing series of acts ever seen during a major-league ball game. He was so bad in the first game that Boudreau wouldn't start him in the second.

He went through all his old antics, and added a number of new ones. During the game, while the Red Sox pitcher was warming up, he started doing a hula-hula dance, and the customers behind him responded with a chorus that sounded like a thousand ukeleles strumming. Piersall got a fluke hit off Saul Rogovin, the Chicago pitcher, when the ball hit his bat as he was ducking away, and then he ran out to right field at the end of the inning, flexing his muscles like a professional strong man. When Ray Scarborough was sent to relieve Willard Nixon, the Red Sox starting pitcher, in the fifth inning, Scarborough rode to the mound from the bull pen in a jeep. As it passed Piersall he put up his thumb trying to hitch-hike a ride. He did it again when Bill Henry rode by to relieve Scarborough. The fans loved it.

Aside from the clowning, Piersall did well in the ball

game. He was the only man on the Red Sox to get two hits off Rogovin, who won 7–2. Piersall made several good catches, and two throws that according to the stories in the scrapbook were outstanding. Twenty minutes after the game was over, Boudreau said, "Vollmer is my right fielder." Piersall started the game on the bench, but later he wandered out to the bull pen, which in Chicago is next to the right-field foul line.

Vollmer played most of the game, but Boudreau sent word for Piersall to replace him in the ninth. Dutch came out from the dugout to get his glove at the same moment that Piersall dashed out from the bull pen. Before taking his setting-up exercises and going through the routine of giving the fans the full treatment, Piersall made a circus catch of the sunglasses which Vollmer tossed to him, then turned and bowed while the crowd in his corner of the grandstand roared. Later that inning he robbed Chico Carrasquel of the White Sox of a double with a spectacular catch that ended the game, and as he ran into the locker room, he kept turning and bowing to the screaming fans.

Warren Brown, the *Chicago Herald-American* sports columnist, wrote the next day:

"While the young man may never reach the batting heights nor collect salary checks proportionate to those which went Ted Williams's way, young Jim Piersall, the Red Sox eccentric, continues to make his pitch as perhaps the game's most distinctive crowd-pleaser.

"Comiskey Park fans, all over the park, were completely captivated by Piersall's antics in the first game.

When he finally appeared in the last inning of the second game, the ovation he got was as great as anything ever accorded a Williams or a Joe DiMaggio by a crowd whose sympathies figured to be with the home team.

"General Manager Frank Lane of the [White] Sox, conceding that Piersall is not only an excellent ballplayer now, but has unlimited potentialities, said he had encountered young Jim under the stands before the double-header began. Piersall was on his way from the clubhouse to the field.

" 'Hi, Mr. Lane,' said Piersall, 'I want to ask you something. Why do you go around giving those big bonuses for kid ballplayers? Why don't you give Mr. [Tom] Yawkey [owner of the Red Sox] one hundred and fifty thousand dollars and get me? Then you'd really have something.'

"The best Lane could say to that was to tell Piersall to go ahead and arrange the deal.

"On the White Sox's last trip to Boston, [Manager] Paul Richards was seated in a corner of the Kenmore Hotel lobby when a gangling youngster came rushing up, wanted to know how things were going, rattled off a lot of conversation, didn't give Richards a chance to reply, and went darting down the steps and into the street.

" 'Who,' I asked Richards, 'might that be?'

" 'That,' said Richards, 'is Piersall. Wish I had him.' "

The Boston newspapers jumped down Boudreau's throat for benching Piersall. Reluctant to admit that it was because of the clowning, Lou announced that he had done it because Piersall wasn't hitting and he thought Vollmer might shake loose into another streak. The only trouble with that argument was that Piersall had been hitting very well, and Vollmer, after replacing Piersall, remained in a slump. The Red Sox went from Chicago to St. Louis and drew twenty-one thousand fans in two nights there. Piersall got into two of the three games in the late innings, and went through his repertoire, but Boudreau kept him out of the third game altogether. He benched Vollmer, too. Charley Maxwell played right field for the Red Sox that day.

Boudreau put Piersall back in the lineup when the Red Sox got to Cleveland for a four-game series with the Indians. He played right field throughout the series, but the Red Sox lost three of the games and Piersall put on another comprehensive clowning act during the Sunday doubleheader that ended the Cleveland stay. His style was a little cramped in Cleveland, because the stands at the Municipal Stadium are some distance away from right field, and there was no one for him to yell to. However, he attracted enough attention to be the central figure of the afternoon, and Boudreau benched him again in Detroit. Vollmer was back in right field, but Piersall got into every game, and, back in a ball park where the fans could talk to him, he gave the customers everything he had. Then the Red Sox came home to Boston to open a series against Washington on the night of Friday, June 27.

"Holy cow," I said to Mary, "I was worse in the West than I had been in Boston."

"You were pretty bad, honey, so bad that I went out to see if I couldn't quiet you down."

"You mean you made that trip with us?"

"Part of it. I had to."

"Why?"

"Partly because I wanted to talk to Boudreau about you, but mostly because I wanted everyone on the ball club to know that I hadn't left you."

I stared at her.

"To know *what?*"

She nodded.

"That's right, honey. You told everyone that I had walked out on you."

On the morning of the day the Red Sox left for the Western trip, Mary, scared and upset herself, started out for Scranton, where she intended to stay while we were on the road. The children and Ann, Mary's sister, were with her. Mary kissed me good-by when I left for the ball park, and then left town. A few days after she arrived in Scranton, she got a call from Jim Tracy, who, in common with his brothers Bill and Frank, had been in and out of Boston all season trying to straighten me out. He had been at Fenway Park for the last game of our home stand, and one of the Red Sox ballplayers asked him if it was true that Mary had left me.

"That's when I decided to go to Cleveland," she said. "I had been thinking about making the trip anyhow. The Scranton papers were full of your antics in Chicago, and when Boudreau benched you, they had it all over Page

One. I thought maybe if I could talk to Boudreau, it would help."

Mary met me in Cleveland, and we stayed a couple of nights at the hotel and one with Ethel and George Minnicucci, some friends of ours who had moved there from Waterbury. But Mary didn't get to talk to Boudreau at all, and didn't even see him until we got on the train to Detroit. We were in the dining car that evening, and Boudreau was sitting at a nearby table with the coaches. They didn't know we were so close by, and Mary overheard them talking about me.

"They were all so upset and puzzled over the way you acted that I didn't have to ask Boudreau what he thought about you," she said. "I realized then that he didn't have any more idea how to handle you than I did. Besides, he had so much on his mind that I didn't want to add mine to his collection of worries. I never did speak to him about you."

Mary didn't stay in Detroit for the whole series. Instead, she took the train back to Scranton. There she picked up the children and then drove to Boston with her father. She arrived late on the night of the twenty-seventh, the same night that we opened our home stand against Washington. It was also the night that I outdid myself to a point where it was obvious that something would have to be done to get me back into line. I went through all the old gags for the fans, twenty-six thousand of whom flocked out to the ball park that night, and I invented plenty of new ones. But because Vollmer started the game, I had to cram most of my action into the practice session that preceded it. Bob Addie, of the *Washington Times-Herald*, devoted his column to my activities that night. Here, in part, is what he wrote:

"There have been few rookies in all baseball history who commanded as much attention as James Anthony Piersall, a twenty-two-year-old product of Waterbury, Connecticut, heretofore known chiefly for its watchmaking. In the case of J. A. Piersall, the inference has been that there was something wrong with the works.

"Before the Washington Nats were to play the Red Sox, Boston was taking batting practice. As is usual in those cases, the opposing team was on the bench waiting its turn.

"The Nats were all seated in the dugout when Piersall gave a special performance of his gifted clowning ability — while parrying barbed insults from the Washington players.

"Piersall would see a pop fly coming, stagger under it and then make it miss his head by a fraction of an inch. He was stopping ground balls with his feet and looked like Nick Altrock at the latter's clowning best.

"In fielding practice, Piersall was playing second base. Del Wilber was catching while Manager Lou Boudreau was hitting grounders. Piersall fielded the ball, threw to the plate, then ran to second base, lay prone on the ground and stuck his glove over his head. He caught Wilber's relay from the plate as easily as if he had been five feet away.

"When Clyde Vollmer, who took over the right-field position from Piersall, was at the plate in the batting practice, Piersall kept up a running comment for the benefit of the Washington players.

" 'I'm Vollmer's caddie,' he said. 'If he gets hot, I'll never get back into the lineup.'

"Out in center field, a group of bleacherites unfurled a banner reading, 'We want Piersall.' Jim acknowledged his followers before the game began, then went into the dugout because Vollmer started.

"With one out in the seventh inning and the Sox in the field, Boudreau suddenly inserted Piersall in right field. He went out there like a returning war hero. The crowd went wild.

"You would have thought the Sox kept Piersall tied in a sack because it took him longer to unkink than any man I've ever seen. He took calisthenics. He imitated the pitcher [Sid Hudson]. He mimicked the batter, Jackie Jensen. There was a foul hit into the stands back of first base. From thirty yards away Piersall, who had no more chance of catching the ball than I did from the press box, came tearing in. He was all over that field. When the inning was over, Piersall trotted in behind Dom DiMaggio."

Addie went on to describe my imitation of DiMaggio's gait, and repeated some of the other stories concerning my activities of the previous month. Then he wrote:

"Piersall's teammates, from all that can be gathered, greet his hi-jinks with cold fury. Yet the fans and the press love him because he is so colorful. The newspapermen in Boston talk of Piersall as one speaks of an incorrigible child, tsk-tsking some of his exploits yet taking pride in his deviltry."

Aside from everything that Addie described, I apparently did something else that night that caused a great deal of unrest in the ball club and, when it was disclosed, a tremendous amount of discussion around the baseball circuit. It seems that I was in the Red Sox locker room changing my shirt when Vern Stephens's four-year-old son walked in. According to the stories I read, I reached out, spanked him and sent him screeching down the runway to his father, who was in the dugout.

I know I did a lot of unusual things during this period, but I'm positive that I never spanked either Stephens's or anyone else's child. I might have — and probably did — give him a little pat on the flank, but I suppose I'll never be able to prove it. I don't remember, the child was too young to say anything one way or the other and nobody else happened to be in the locker room at the time. However, the story did break several days later and I am quoted as saying that I patted the child lightly, which is enough to convince me that that's all I did. Stephens evidently is also convinced, because he has since told me that his boy cried simply because I was a stranger to him and that there is no question that I neither spanked him nor hit him very hard. However, in the light of what happened within the next sixteen hours, I don't suppose anyone can be blamed for what was said or written about me.

At midnight, after the June 27 game with Washington was over, Boudreau announced to the press, "From now on, Piersall's my right fielder."

The next morning, he called me into his office and

told me that the Red Sox had decided to send me to Birmingham.

Here, in part, is the way Roger Birtwell, a Boston baseball writer, told the story in the July 9, 1952, issue of the *Sporting News:*

"Jim Piersall — at twenty-two — is without question one of the best fielding and throwing outfielders in the game today. With the Red Sox, he batted .296 — one hit under .300 — for all the games he started as an outfielder.

"Yet the Red Sox, in a startling move late in the morning of Saturday, June 28, demoted Piersall to their Double A farm club at Birmingham. The big-league career of one of the most talented and colorful players in the game's history had been sliced to ten and a half weeks. And part of that time was spent on the bench.

"Less than twelve hours before, Manager Lou Boudreau had announced that Piersall would return from the bench and resume his place at right field for the Red Sox.

" 'Piersall's attitude was detrimental to this club,' was Boudreau's explanation of Jim's assignment to Birmingham. 'I have to consider twenty-five or thirty other ballplayers — plus trying to win.'

"Said General Manager Joe Cronin: 'Apparently everyone on this club is against him [Piersall]. There really was a bad situation down on the bench and in the clubhouse.'

"Boudreau revealed that he called Piersall into the manager's office at the Red Sox clubhouse at ten-thirty A.M. and said, 'Jim, you've been optioned to Birmingham.

I want you to quiet down, and I want you to improve your hitting.'

"The move was like sending Shakespeare out to write obituaries on a country weekly.

"At the airport, before taking off, the twenty-two-year-old right fielder made a few remarks of his own.

" 'Vollmer can't even blow his nose,' exclaimed Piersall.

" 'McKechnie is running the Red Sox; Boudreau isn't,' was another Piersall exclamation. [This reference was to Bill McKechnie, then a Red Sox coach.]

" 'There isn't anyone on the club playing better than I am except George Kell,' added Piersall. 'And he likes to win, too.' "

I looked up from the scrapbook, and Mary was watching me.

"Did I do all that?" I demanded. "Did I say all that?"

"You must have. The newspapers all quoted you the same way."

"McKechnie and Boudreau and Cronin and everyone else around the Red Sox must have been ready to murder me."

"I don't know," Mary said. "I guess by then they were just glad to get rid of you. I can't say as I blame them."

"Neither can I. But how about you?"

"I was scared — scared to death. I knew there was something terribly wrong, and I was afraid of where it might lead you. There was only one thing that looked promising —"

Then she told me that, after I had been told about going to Birmingham, I had phoned her, and, although, I was deeply depressed, I talked logically about how I was going to handle myself.

"Those people want me to settle down," I told her. "And that's just what I'm going to do. I'll concentrate on baseball, and when the Red Sox are convinced that I'm all right, they'll take me back."

"No more clowning?" Mary said.

"No more clowning. I'm going to behave myself. I've got to get back to Boston."

Then I went home and wired Garrett Wall, my closest friend in Birmingham. We had spent a lot of time with him in 1951. He was a redhead who worked for a trucking company, a hot baseball fan and a real nice guy. I asked him to meet me at the Birmingham airport and drive me to the ball park, since I would arrive just in time to get into that night's game for a few innings.

I wouldn't let Mary drive me to the Boston airport. My parents, who had been in town for a few days, were driving back to Waterbury, so I had them take me to the airport first. When I said good-by to Mary and the children, I told her not to plan to go to Birmingham.

"I'll be back before you know it," I said.

Mary felt pretty good when I left the house, since I promised her over and over I'd behave myself. But then, when she read what I had said at the airport, she gave up any hope that things in Birmingham would be any better than they had been in Boston.

My 1952 Birmingham debut was similar to the start I had there in 1951. Instead of driving in with Mary, I flew in, and instead of coming from Louisville, I was coming from Boston. But in both cases, I rushed to the ball park the minute I arrived in town, and got there in time to get into the game that night. Wall met me and drove me to Rickwood Field, where the Barons played their home games.

The Barons had a new manager, Red Mathis, who was also the team's catcher. I knew him well, since I had played with him the year before. He was another carrot-top — his hair was a real flaming red. A stocky, powerful man, he was a friendly guy who, in his first year as a manager, was very anxious to make good. When I walked into the dugout he put me right into the ball game. Miraculously, I hit the first ball pitched to me over the left-field fence for a home run.

When the game was over that night, I got Joe Cronin out of bed with a long-distance phone call to Boston and told him all about what a great game I'd played.

My ears burned when I read that in the scrapbook. I put it down and said, "I must have been in very bad shape. One minute I'd be perfectly logical and the next minute completely haywire."

"The spells of logic had everybody fooled," she replied, "and nobody wanted to be fooled more than I. I put too much stock in them myself — otherwise, I would have insisted that the Red Sox send you to a doctor instead of shipping you to Birmingham."

"I was real bad in Birmingham?"

"You were pretty bad, honey. Worse than you had been here."

I was with the Barons exactly twenty days. During that

time, I had countless arguments with the umpires. I was thrown out of half a dozen ball games and suspended four different times. I baffled my teammates, infuriated my manager, insulted the umpires, squabbled with opposing ballplayers and delighted the sports writers and fans. Once I nearly got into an open fist fight. Twice, at my own expense, I flew back to Boston.

At first, the Birmingham baseball people welcomed my clowning. Eddie Glennon, the Barons general manager, announced a few days after my arrival that I had injected new spirit into the team. "He's the greatest center fielder that I've ever seen," Glennon said. "A one-hundred-and-fifty-thousand-dollar ballplayer." I added color to the Barons and made them the talk of the Southern Association — indeed, the talk of baseball. Every unconventional move I made was relayed to the nation's newspapers and splashed all over the sports pages.

But it didn't take long for everyone, including Glennon, to get sick and tired of Piersall. He was funny only as long as he added something refreshing to the ball game. But when he tried to make his antics take the place of the ball game, he was in trouble. His clowning was turning games into travesties. He did stupid little things — anything he could think of — to delay the games, and the angry umpires, anxious to hustle things up, reached a point where they had to banish him in order to get contests completed at all.

Piersall put on one of his most aggravating performances in New Orleans on July 5. Aside from going through the regular routine which had first attracted attention when he was in the majors, Piersall added a whole new bag of tricks, making them up as he went along. When he went up to hit, he stood in the batter's box, dropped his bat and imitated the pitcher as he wound up. Naturally, the umpire had to call time, and the game would be held up while Piersall stooped to pick up his war club. He pulled the stunt two or three times each time he came up.

When Piersall wasn't imitating the pitcher, he was holding up the works while he ran either down the first- or the third-base line to give instructions in a dramatic stage whisper to one of the coaches or to a base runner. Sometimes he rushed back to the dugout to talk to Mathis, who repeatedly ordered him to get back up there and hit.

After Birmingham's turn at bat, Piersall loafed his way out to center field, stopping to talk to infielders on the way, taking his time about picking up his glove, sauntering over near the stands to exchange quips with the crowd and spending so much time reaching his position that the game had to be held up while an umpire came out to hustle him up. Once while New Orleans was at bat, Piersall suddenly ran into the Birmingham dugout from his center-field position and the game had to be stopped. Mathis, who was catching, had to leave his position to come over and tell Piersall to get back on the job.

About halfway through the game, one of the Barons hit what Mathis thought was a home run, and when the umpire called it a foul ball, Red blew his top. He rushed over to George Popp, the plate umpire, yelling and gesticulating — and Piersall rushed right behind him, imitating every move he made. Mathis got so excited that Popp finally threw him out of the game. Piersall didn't stop aping Red until he turned around to go into the locker room.

When Birmingham's half of the inning was over, Piersall went out to the pitcher's mound, picked up the ball, and walked out to the shortstop's position. When Johnny McCall, the Barons pitcher, came out to warm up, he yelled to Piersall to throw the ball. Piersall wound up and slammed it right at McCall. McCall had to put up his gloved hand fast to keep from getting hit in the face. Boiling mad, McCall threw the ball right back at Piersall, who fell flat on his face, then got up holding his stomach in mock hysterics after the ball had sailed to the outfield.

The crowd laughed, but neither McCall nor Popp thought it was very funny. Popp came halfway out on the diamond and called to Piersall, "Go out and get that ball in here before I throw you out of the game." The ball had stopped in dead center field. Piersall dropped his glove on the ground and kicked it as he went along. Just before he reached the ball, he crouched and crept towards it as though he were a pointer dog and it were his quarry. Then he kicked it a few feet, and kept repeating the performance until the ball and he had reached the scoreboard.

Piersall finally picked it up and threw it to the scoreboard boy, who threw it back. They began playing catch, but that game didn't last long. All of the umpires at once were screaming at Piersall to get out of the ball game.

When the scoreboard boy refused to throw the ball back, Piersall walked off the field.

Then, still in uniform, he wandered over to the right-field side of the grandstand, where five hundred boys, guests of Joe L. Brown, the president of the New Orleans club, were chanting, "We want Piersall!" Piersall stood in front of them and led them in the cheers. Somehow they got the game started again on the field, but nobody was watching. Everyone was looking over at Piersall.

Finally, he went down to the Birmingham locker room and changed into street clothes. Then he went back to the stands and sat down in a box occupied by Charles Hurth, the president of the Southern Association. From there, Piersall heckled Popp, as well as Danny Murtaugh, the New Orleans manager, who had been giving him a pretty rough going-over all through the game. For that performance he was suspended.

A few days later, everyone in the league had four days off while the Southern Association all-star game was being played. I hopped a plane and flew back to Boston, wiring Mary ahead of time. I thought that the Red Sox might let me stay with them, once I was in Boston. But when I called Cronin, he told me to go back to the Barons and stick to baseball. I left the next day.

By this time, Glennon was worried about me, too. He persuaded me to let him take me to a doctor in Birmingham, and I was given some pills to calm me down. I behaved all right for a day or so, but then I went off again worse than ever. We were starting a long home stand, and the Birmingham fans and I were enjoying each other hugely. The only trouble was, nobody else was enjoying me.

I became worse and worse. Nobody could keep me under control, including the umpires. One night I stood at the plate and screamed over a called third strike, and when the umpire thumbed me out of the game, I pulled a water pistol out of my pocket, squirted the plate with it and said, "Now maybe you can see it." I drew another suspension for that, my fourth since I had arrived in Birmingham.

It looked as if I were going to be stuck there for the season, so I decided to go back to Boston to get Mary and the children. Up to that point they hadn't moved South because we always had the hope that I'd get back to the Red Sox any day. They kept the house in Newton while I stayed with Garrett Wall in Birmingham.

Garrett had had no more luck trying to settle me down than anyone else had. He was placed in a position similar to that of Ted Lepcio when I was with the Red Sox. Like Mary, they both had to stand by and watch me crack up, doing what they could by talking to me but not daring to go much further, in the desperate hope that I might get straightened out by myself. Every morning when they got up, they were saying to themselves, "This might be the day." And every night they went to bed, thinking, "Maybe tomorrow."

I bought a ticket on a Boston plane that left Birmingham late in the afternoon of July 17. We made several stops on the way, including one at LaGuardia Airport in New York, where Bill Cunningham, the able *Boston*

Herald sports columnist, and his secretary, Miss Frances Donovan, got aboard. Apparently, as soon as I saw Cunningham, I rushed over to him and began pouring my troubles into his unwilling ear. Evidently I talked all the way to Boston, where we arrived at one-thirty in the morning. Here, in part, is what he wrote in his column a day or so later:

"I chanced to be on the plane that unexpectedly brought the Red Sox problem child Jimmy Piersall into Boston at one-thirty A.M. From approximately eleven-forty-five P.M. until the ship set down in Boston, I'd heard little but the machine-gun chatter of this tormented youth who so foolishly is throwing away a promising career . . .

"It's my considered opinion that the less written now the better, and if anybody's really interested in helping the young man, a complete press blackout until he can get his bearings would be the best medicine that could possibly be prescribed.

"I'm no authority on such matters, but my guess is he's heading straight for a nervous breakdown."

Cunningham was an accurate prophet. My breakdown was just around the corner. It happened within forty hours after I arrived in Boston. And, suffering more pangs than I suffered, living more horrible minutes than I lived, fighting more fights than I fought, sinking farther into depths of desperation than I sank, hoping more than I hoped, and praying more than I prayed was Mary. I went through it all under the unhealthy anesthesia of a mental blackout. Mary was fully aware of everything that went on. She carried me through every step of the way without so much as a sleeping pill — and, to this day, she remembers every dreadful minute. She told me all about it during those days when we sat quietly in our rented house and relived the past together.

The house was alive with reporters and photographers the day after I flew into town from Birmingham. All of the papers, the major press services, the radio and television stations — every conceivable dispenser of news — sent out representatives. Everyone interviewed me, and while I reveled in the prospects of so much publicity, I was reasonable and rational in my speech. I told them all the same story — that I was through with clowning, and from that moment on, was going to be no more and no less than a ballplayer. I said that I would go back to Birmingham and do the best I could to help the Barons win the Southern Association pennant, and that my one hope was to get back to the Red Sox as soon as possible. And once with them, I would forget all about these mad antics.

I parried the embarrassing questions —

"Did you spank Stephens's little boy?" . . . Of course not — I just patted him, that's all. . . . "Did you really calm down the way Boudreau told you to?" . . . Certainly. . . . "What about all those stories of your tearing through the Southern Association the way you tore through the American League?" . . . Nothing to them — I've just been sticking to baseball. . . . "Are you really carrying on a running feud with the umpires down there?" . . . Not that I know of — the umpires and me have been getting along fine. . . . "Is it true that you mimicked your own manager behind his back while he was protesting a decision?" . . . Absolutely not — my manager is a close friend of mine. . . . "Did you squirt the plate with a water pistol?" . . . Someone dreamed that one up. . . . "And play catch with a scoreboard boy?" . . . I should say not. . . . "Why did you make two trips back to Boston in less than three weeks?" . . . To see my family. . . . "Are you going to take your wife and children back to Birmingham?" . . . As soon as I can get them packed and out of here. . . . "Do you really think McKechnie and not Boudreau is running the Red Sox?" . . . Boudreau is the manager — do you think I'd say anything like that? . . . "Well, did you say it?" . . . I was sore — I didn't know what I was talking about — Boudreau runs the team, not McKechnie. . . . "And how about Vollmer — did you say he couldn't blow his nose?" . . . A fine ballplayer and a good friend of mine — why should I say anything to hurt him? . . . "Is it true that some of the Red Sox wanted to beat you up on a train and Lepcio stopped them?" . . . I don't know — ask Lepcio. . . .

All day and all evening that sort of thing went on. Questions, questions, questions — one interviewer after another. Sometimes there would be slight variations, but in general the questions were the same. Mary hovered in and out of the living room while I held court. Every so often, she would suggest that I be excused from answering any more questions, but I wouldn't stand for it. I insisted on seeing everyone and answering everything.

Late that afternoon, the Red Sox office called. Cronin

wanted to see me. He would expect me in his office at ten o'clock the next morning. I had a long talk with him, then went home and said to Mary, "I'm going to see a doctor. They want you there, too." We drove back to the ball park, where Cronin met us, and then we headed for the doctor's.

Before we sat down, the doctor called in another doctor, and then the five of us — the two doctors, Cronin, Mary and I — went into a long huddle. The conversation was pretty general, as if we were all just passing the time of day, and I took part in it. After a while, one of the doctors suggested, "I think it would be a good idea for Jimmy to go off somewhere for a rest."

"Rest?" I asked suspiciously. "What kind of rest?"

"Oh, just a little vacation from baseball. I'd like to see you sitting back and forgetting everything for a while."

"Do I need that kind of a rest?"

"I think you could use one," said the doctor.

"Where can I go?"

"I know just the place for you — it's quiet and restful — an hour out of the city — not too hard for your wife to reach when she goes to see you."

"What do you mean — not too hard for her to reach?" I snapped. "Isn't she going to be with me?"

"You've got to get away from everything, Jimmy," the doctor said. "Even your family."

"Now, wait a minute — what kind of a place is this? It sounds like a hospital."

"It's not exactly a hospital — it's more like a rest home."

I jumped and shouted, "I don't need any rest — and I'm not going to any hospital."

Nobody moved. Then one of the doctors said, quietly, "All right, Jimmy, calm down. Nobody is going to send you anywhere you don't want to go. We just want to help you."

I relaxed and shrugged my shoulders. Then, without sitting down, I said, "I know. Can I talk to my wife alone for a few minutes?"

"Of course."

The three men left the room, and Mary and I talked. Gently, she tried to persuade me to do what the doctors wanted, but I wouldn't listen at first. The very word "hospital" was enough to set me off again. I wanted no part of any hospitals.

"What difference does it make what you call the place?" Mary said. "You need a rest. Let the doctors decide where you should go to get one."

"No hospital," I said, stubbornly.

"Not for me?"

I said nothing.

"Jimmy, honey —"

"What?"

"If you won't do it for me — will you do it for our babies?"

I looked at her and shrugged my shoulders. She went to the door and called the doctors and Cronin back into the room.

"Before I say yes or no," I insisted, "I want to know what kind of a place I'm going to, how much freedom

[183]

I'll have when I get there and how long I'll have to stay."

The doctors told me that I would probably only have to stay for three weeks at the most, and that I would have plenty of freedom to come and go as I pleased. I asked Mary again, and she urged me to go. Cronin added that the Red Sox were very much in favor of my going away, and he assured me that my salary would continue to be sent to Mary while I was gone.

"The club will pay all the bills in connection with this," he said. "We want you to be in the best possible physical condition so that when you start playing ball again, you'll have nothing else on your mind."

I finally agreed, and we went out. It was a long ride to the private sanitarium where I was to go, and Mary, who was worried and exhausted, was strongly urged not to drive me there. The place is in a small community in the northern part of the state about an hour and a half from where we lived in Newton. I finally agreed, after some argument, to let someone else drive me, and Joe Cronin arranged for my transportation.

I was permitted to do pretty much as I pleased after I got there. I could use the recreation room, I could wander around the grounds and I was told that I would even be allowed to go into the town provided I got back at a specified hour. Still, I was suspicious of the place. It certainly looked like a hospital to me. I walked out the day after I went in. Mary was called, and she drove right up there. When she arrived, the doctors told her that I had refused to take a shot and had taken off while the nurse had gone to get help. They couldn't find me around the town and thought I'd probably gone home. Mary turned around and drove back to Newton.

The phone rang just as she walked into the house. It was the sanitarium again. I had just phoned the sanitarium from a pay station — probably in Boston — and told them that I was going back there. Mary got into the car and drove back again. Fifteen minutes after she arrived at the place, I walked in.

We greeted each other casually, and then I said, "How about a game of table tennis?"

We played a few sets, and then she kissed me good-by and drove home. At about noon the next day, she got another call. I had walked out again after refusing to take a shot. I still hadn't come back when Mary got there, so she decided to look around the town for me, rather than sit around the hospital and sweat out my return.

She found me passing the time of day with a couple of other guys in the shed of a gas station. The others hadn't recognized me and we weren't on the subject of baseball. When I saw Mary, I got up casually and went over to say hello to her. She got me into the car and, after some discussion, persuaded me to let her drive me back to the sanitarium.

Back in the recreation room, we played some more table tennis and shot a couple of games of pool together, and then it was time for dinner. Mary left, and promised to be back later. She had a bite to eat in town, and was back within an hour, but in that hour the world fell apart.

Once again, an attempt had been made to give me a shot, and again I had refused. Two attendants came in later and I still refused, and the more they insisted, the louder I became. After a while I lost my head altogether and began swinging and fighting and yelling and screaming, so they had to go out and get help. By the time Mary returned, the police had been called, and I had been the central figure in a wild, free-for-all fight, during which I had gone completely out of control. Because of my condition, I was immediately ordered transferred to the state mental institution at Danvers.

The doctors broke the news as gently as possible to Mary. "We aren't equipped to handle him here," they told her. "That's why we have to have him shifted. He's been pretty violent."

Mary hung around the sanitarium until they moved me out of there, but I didn't recognize her and she hardly recognized me. I was securely tied down, and my eyes were puffed, my face bloody and my clothes torn. They got me into an ambulance and roared off while Mary, now frantic with fear, helplessly stood by and tried not to look.

On her way home, she noticed a sign pointing to the Danvers State Hospital and, even though it was after midnight, she turned off the main road and drove up to the front office. There, she was told that there was no point in her staying around any longer — that they'd do all they could for me and that I probably would be all right. The next day they transferred me to Westborough.

"Holy cow!" I exclaimed, after she told me the story. "How did you stand it?"

She shrugged and smiled a little.

"You know, honey," she said, "I think we're all built to stand almost anything. If you told me now that I'd have to go through it all again tomorrow, I wouldn't be able to stand the thought of it. Every night when I went to bed praying that you would be all right, I prayed for strength myself — not just physical strength, but the strength to carry me through this thing. I was never sure how much more I'd be able to take, yet I got by all right."

"I couldn't have stood it," I said.

"Yes, you could — if you had to."

I FELT so good when I got home from Westborough that I called Joe Cronin and asked him if I could make the last Western trip with the Red Sox. They had already left Boston and were in Detroit. Cronin didn't think it was such a good idea and told me so.

"The season's almost over anyhow, Jimmy," he said. "I think it would be better for you to pass this one up. And I'll bet your doctor agrees with me."

He was right. Dr. Brown told me later he would never have let me make the trip even if Cronin had given me permission. I saw the doctor three times after I was discharged from the hospital. Each time Mary drove me to Westborough and stayed with us while we talked. The doctor and his wife had a house right on the grounds. I visited him there once, and at his office in one of the hospital buildings the other times.

I was very calm about going back to Westborough.

[187]

"The place isn't exactly my favorite amusement park," I said to Mary, "but I don't mind visiting there."

"Neither do I," she said, "as long as you don't have to stay. But if it bothers you to go, I'll ask Dr. Brown to come here. I'm sure he will."

"No. I want to go. There's nothing to be afraid of."

One thing we wanted to ask him was whether or not it would be all right for me to go to Scranton for Ann O'Brien's wedding. She and Dan Kuchar were getting married the third week in September, and Mary was to be matron of honor. Because of my situation, Mary had suggested that Ann get someone else. But Ann insisted on waiting to see if Mary would be able to make it. Ann and Dan had been going together for a long time — in fact they had an understanding at the time Mary and I first met. They were to be married by Father John O'Brien, Ann's brother, the same priest who had married us.

"By all means, go," Dr. Brown said. "Both of you. It will give Jimmy a chance to mingle with old friends under the most pleasant possible conditions."

Before we left for Scranton, Cronin phoned me one day and said, "How would you like to spend the winter in Florida? The Red Sox will pay your expenses."

I almost dropped the phone.

"You mean the whole winter?" I asked.

"Sure. Go down there whenever you feel like it, and stay right through spring training. I'll have Tom Dowd rent a house for you in Sarasota."

Dowd was the Red Sox traveling secretary.

[188]

"Gee — I don't know how to thank you, Mr. Cronin — you and Mr. Yawkey —"

"Forget it. When can you leave?"

I told him about the Scranton trip, so he said, "All right, we'll set it up for October 1."

Mary did all of the driving when we went to Scranton for the Kuchars' wedding. The town looked good to me, even though my last memory of it wasn't a very happy one. The wedding guests were practically all close friends of ours and everyone accepted me as casually as though I had been spending the summer playing ball. Not one person asked me about my illness, for which I was grateful. I had not been among strangers at all since leaving the hospital, and it was the one prospect that bothered me. I wasn't a bit sure I'd know how to react if someone started recalling any of those stunts I had pulled during my illness.

Mary drove us back to Boston a couple of days after the Kuchars were married, and, with only a few days left before it was time to go to Sarasota, we made a last visit to Westborough.

"I'm a little afraid of what's going to happen when we get there," I told the doctor.

"What's there to be afraid of?"

"Well, I'll run into a lot of casual acquaintances and people I don't know. What if they ask me about some of those things I did when I was playing ball?"

"What if they do?"

"Well — what shall I tell them?"

"Tell them the truth. Tell them you don't remember anything that happened. That's simple enough, isn't it?"

"Well — there's another thing —" I said.

"What?"

"Suppose — suppose I can't play ball any more?"

"Jimmy — you're not going to worry about that now."

"But I want to know. I've got to find out if I can still catch a ball, if my arm is still strong, if my baseball instincts are still sharp, if I can hit big-league pitching. How am I going to find out?"

The doctor peered closely at me, his dark eyes snapping. Then he said, "I don't want you to give one minute of your time, to lose one second of your sleep, to worry one single bit about whether or not you'll be able to play baseball. It's a wonderful thing that the Red Sox are doing — sending you to Florida where you can recuperate under the best of conditions. But unless you promise me that you won't touch a baseball, a glove or a bat until it's time to start spring training, I won't let you go."

"But you let me play ball around the grounds while I was here."

"That was different. You were playing with a lot of fellows to whom baseball was simply recreation. It's your profession. If something goes wrong during the winter — or even if you think something is going wrong, it might set you back. I don't want you to play ball all winter. Understand?"

"All right, Doc — if you say so."

"Fine," he said. "Now when you get down there, you eat and sleep and relax and fish and play golf and put on

some flesh. What was your normal playing weight before?"

"About one hundred seventy."

"I'd like to see you playing at about one hundred
ninety. If you sit and stew all winter over what's going
to happen in the spring, you'll never make it. And one
other thing, Jimmy. Be natural and casual with people
you meet. Don't act as if they think you're the star per-
former in a circus sideshow. And remember — if you
need me, I'll still be no farther away from you than the
nearest telephone."

"Can I help Mary drive the car down?" I asked.

"Drive a little — but not more than a hundred miles
at a time. Let Mary do most of it."

Dowd had rented a five-room house for us on East
Goldenrod Street in Sarasota. It was just off the South
Trail, which is part of the Tamiami Trail, the main high-
way between Tampa and Miami. The ball park was about
a mile away, but it might as well have been a thousand.
I didn't go near it.

We were still moving our stuff in from the car when
someone yelled, "Hey, Jimmy —"

I turned, and coming along the side of the house from
the direction of our back yard was George Susce, one of
the Red Sox coaches. He had a huge grin on his face and
he walked towards me with both hands outstretched.

I was delighted to see him. Susce came from Pitts-
burgh, but he had moved to Sarasota the year before. He
looked older than he was, for he had a weatherbeaten,
India-rubber face and his sandy hair was rapidly desert-

ing the top of his head. A chunky man, he was — and still is — one of the best bull-pen catchers in the baseball business. Never an outstanding ballplayer, he had become a coach when Boudreau had managed the Cleveland Indians and moved to the Red Sox later. Susce had a bright, friendly personality, backed up by a ready wit and a genuine interest in people, and everyone liked him.

He was only in his mid-forties, but he was a fatherly sort of guy, and, indeed, he had a son who was just about my age. George was wonderful around rookies, for he loved to work with them, and he had a knack of giving encouragement with such solid sincerity that he could convince the most depressed kid that he had a big-league future.

After we shook hands, I said, "Holy cow, you didn't waste any time coming in to say hello."

"Didn't need much time. I live right over on the next street. All you have to do to get to my house is go through your back yard and cross the road and there you are."

Susce was the perfect neighbor for me. Now I needed the close companionship of a trusted friend with a baseball background, someone who knew the people I knew and who understood how to handle the strangers who knew me. I had received nation-wide publicity for months, and my face was familiar to thousands of fans who had seen pictures of me.

Mary and Dr. Brown and all the others had carried me this far — but another baseball man who could help me figure out the problem of meeting strangers and coping with their natural curiosity about me could carry me well along the rest of the way. Susce filled the bill in every conceivable way. The Red Sox couldn't have found a happier situation for me if they had tried — and I'm still not sure they didn't put me that close to George purposely.

Any apprehensions I might have felt melted the minute I shook hands with this warm, sympathetic man. He knew baseball and its problems and he instinctively understood me and mine. He never forced himself on me, yet he was always around when I needed him most. He pulled me through some situations which I would have found hard to take, and he made all potential problems seem like ABC.

Sarasota is more than just the spring-training headquarters for the Red Sox, who have been going there for many years. It is, in some ways, practically the hub of the baseball universe during the wintertime — or at least, the Eastern hub. Scores of baseball men make their home there, and scores more live in the surrounding communities. I couldn't be in the place very long without running into someone I knew, and I wasn't a bit sure what kind of questions I'd be hit with. After all, I had made a spectacle of myself for half the summer, and those who either knew me only casually or hadn't met me at all would be reminded of it as soon as they saw me.

When I mentioned it to George, he laughed and said, "What do you care what kind of questions people ask you? You can answer anything. Don't give it another thought."

I wanted to play golf, but I was a little fearful about meeting people on the course. Susce took me to the Bobby Jones Club and made me feel at home there. He stood beside me as I was greeted by baseball people whom I knew and fans whom I didn't know. He laughed and joked and made things easy when strangers approached me. That seemed to happen all the time, and, sooner or later, I was bound to run up against a reminder of something unpleasant.

Susce didn't play golf, but he used to walk around the course with me for exercise. Sometimes I played alone and sometimes acquaintances or friends would go around with me. I was never physically alone, because if I had no one to play with George came along. He was with me the day a man I'd never met before came up with one of those recollections I dreaded.

We were in the snack bar of the club one afternoon, and a stranger came over, held out his hand, introduced himself and said, "Say, Jimmy, I've been following your career right along."

"That so?" I asked, pleased.

"Yes, sir. And you've done some of the most wonderfully crazy things I've ever heard of. Say, how in the world did you ever think to bring a water pistol to the ball park so you could squirt the plate with it? What a gag that was!"

Wonderfully crazy things . . . water pistol . . . squirting the plate . . . wonderfully crazy things . . . crazy things . . . crazy . . . crazy . . . crazy . . .

I stiffened and wet my lips and clenched my fists and mumbled something, then turned away. I went and stood off in one corner of the room, so I could be as far away from that guy as possible. Then, as I sulked and continued to clench and unclench my fists, I heard Susce, now at my elbow, snap, "What's the matter with you?"

"Did you hear what that guy said?"

"Sure I heard him."

"Did you hear him talk about crazy things — and ask me about that water-pistol thing?"

"I heard him."

I turned on Susce and, in a low but clear voice, seethed, "Well, I don't have to take that stuff from anybody."

"You don't, eh?"

Susce put his hand on my arm and led me out to the porch. Then, poking his forefinger at my chest, he said, "I thought you were all O.K. again."

"I am."

"Well, you didn't act it in there. You looked like you were going to blow your top."

"Well," I said, "I was mad."

"Why? — because the guy used the word crazy? Isn't that part of the English language? Don't people always use it? Do you expect them to change when they're talking to you?"

"The guy should have known better."

"Maybe he should. But he didn't. Can you get mad at him for that?"

"But, George, did you hear what he asked me?"

"Why shouldn't he ask you?" Susce said. "That water-pistol gag was a beauty — one of the funniest I've ever heard of. A lot of guys are going to ask you about it. They'll ask you about leading cheers for yourself and doing calisthenics in the outfield and hitching rides in the

[195]

bull-pen jeep and playing catch with scoreboard boys and heckling umpires from the president's box and imitating Satchel Paige and all the other things you did while you were sick. And why shouldn't they? You might have forgotten all that, but you can't expect everyone else to. You'll run into a million people who saw you or heard about you and never realized you were sick — don't even know you were in the hospital. Are you going to blow your stack every time one of them says something about those stunts of yours? You'd better not, boy — because you'll be blowing your stack too often for your own good.

"Look, Jimmy" — he was talking softly now — "I'm glad this thing happened. It had to happen sooner or later. It's going to happen again — and it will keep on happening as long as you play ball — maybe for the rest of your life. You've got to accept it, just the way you've learned to accept everything else. But don't let it throw you."

He's right, of course. This is going to happen often. I've got to learn to take it. What was it the doc said — "You can cope with anything" — well, I'll cope with this. I'm going to meet a lot of people who will ask questions like that guy asked me. I can't blame any of them. I'd probably do the same thing myself.

That night I prayed that I might keep my temper, no matter what anyone said to me, and I prayed just as hard for that as I always prayed for everything else — that I'd never be sick again and that I'd be able to play ball as well as I ever had and that Mary and the children would always be safe and well.

[196]

One day, just before spring training began, I asked Susce if he thought I could make the Red Sox ball club.

"You've got it made already," he said. "You're going to be the right fielder."

"But suppose I've lost my touch? Suppose I can't catch a fly ball any more? Suppose I can't throw? Suppose I haven't got that instinct any more — that ability to know just where I should throw the ball, to know just what the best play to make is? And suppose I can't hit?"

"You're the right fielder," he insisted.

"How do you know? You're not the manager."

"Don't worry, I *know*."

"Did Boudreau tell you?"

"Jimmy — don't ask me any more questions. Just take my word for it — you'll be the Red Sox right fielder this year."

He repeated it a dozen times a day in the next few weeks. He said it in my back yard and on his front porch and on the golf course and everywhere else we went together. When it was time to report for spring training, he had me convinced. I checked into Payne Field absolutely certain that I would be the regular Red Sox right fielder for 1953.

I was in perfect physical condition and, just as Dr. Brown advised, I had put on twenty pounds. When I stepped on the scales I weighed one hundred ninety-two pounds. I felt good and couldn't wait to get out on the field to see if I was still a major-league ballplayer.

The other Red Sox players treated me exactly as they treated each other. When ballplayers meet to begin spring training, the general reaction is the same as it is when any group of men, closely knit for part of the year and separated for the rest of it, come together to renew their association. There's always a lot of hand shaking and back slapping and kidding around and shouting back and forth. I was included in all of it. As far as the boys were concerned, I was a routine ballplayer who had had a routine winter vacation.

Everyone I'd played with who was still with the club acted the same towards me. The boys were neither too hot nor too cold. There was no self-conscious moving in, shaking hands and moving out again. I was one of the crowd and that was just the way I wanted it. Even when I saw McDermott for the first time, I felt no embarrassment. He shook hands and kidded with me just as the others had. The same thing happened with Martin when I saw him later in nearby St. Petersburg, where the Yankees trained. The flareups of the year before were forgotten. We met in the natural course of events, shook hands as any two people would after not having seen each other for some time, and passed the time of day.

I was a little concerned about how the umpires would treat me. After all, I had given them a worse going-over than anyone else. Umpires have spring training just the way ballplayers do. Usually an umpire is assigned to a team for several weeks at a time. Bill Summers, a rolypoly veteran who had been around for years, was with us.

When we met for the first time, he held out his hand and said, "How are you doing, Jimmy?"

"Fine," I told him.

"You look great. Now just get out there and stay loose and you'll be all right. Don't worry about anything. Play the best ball you can. The umpires all want to help you. They'll do anything they can to make it easy for you."

Charley Berry, another veteran American League umpire, who joined us later, told me the same thing. Everywhere we played, the umpires who were working the game went out of their way to be nice to me. I was a little apprehensive about Honochick, with whom I'd had that terrible battle in New York, and Passarella, whose conscience I had once challenged, but they were just like the rest.

One umpire even said, "Don't be afraid to squawk if you think we missed a call. No one's trying to muzzle you. If a protest is legitimate, you're entitled to make one. But don't squawk just for the sake of squawking. That's what gets the boys mad."

The newspapermen were wonderful. I read all the Boston papers daily, and I didn't see a single reference to any of the stunts I had pulled either on or off the field, or to the nature of my illness. There was nothing but encouragement, as the baseball writers, to a man, reported how well I was hitting and fielding and how certain it was that I was on my way towards making a sensationally successful comeback.

After the first week of the training season, I began to get heavy mail, most of it from absolute strangers, all of it heartwarming and sincere. Everyone seemed to be wishing me nothing but the very best of good luck.

"They're all with me," I said to Mary. "How can I miss?"

"You can't," she replied. "You're doing fine, honey."

There was still one gnawing fear in my heart. *What about the fans?* The baseball people — players, coaches, managers, umpires, writers — were all co-operating to give me a break, but that's the way baseball people are. Fans come from all walks of life. Most of them figured to give me the best of it — but somebody, somewhere was bound to start yelling insults at me from the stands. *And what will I do then?*

As it turned out, I had to wait a long time to test this situation, for the fans were as wonderful to me as everyone else. We opened the 1953 season in Washington, then went to Philadelphia, then home to Boston, then to Detroit on the first leg of a Western swing and finally to Cleveland before I heard an unkind word from the stands. At the Municipal Stadium in Cleveland, one guy got on me but I managed to ignore him. He didn't start riding me until late in the game, and I could take him or leave him. At that point, I could leave him.

But I was bothered by some of the things he said, and concerned over what might happen when we returned to Cleveland on our next trip. No one else anywhere, even in Chicago, had shown anything but the utmost consideration for me. There was a little flareup in Detroit, when one of the players rode me, but that had no effect on my nerves. The only thing I wanted to find out was just how much I could take from the stands.

On our second trip into Cleveland, I made a spectacular catch, and a guy in the stands yelled down, "Hey, screwball, look out for the man in the white suit!"

Mr. Yawkey had just torn up my contract and given me a new one at a salary raise. I turned around to the guy in the stands and yelled, "How would you like to make the dough this screwball's making?"

A roar of laughter drowned out the heckler's voice, and that was the last I heard from him that afternoon. Ever since then, I've been able to take anything, although, even now, I get very little of that sort of heavy humor from the stands.

My fears about whether or not I could play big-league ball were still gnawing — although vaguely — when we opened the season in Philadelphia. We had to wait two days, because of rainouts. We finally played on April 16, and I got two hits. I had another hit the next day in Philadelphia, and I was beginning to get some confidence in myself. From then on, I managed to get by at the plate, but, aside from the fact that I was coming back, I didn't attract any real attention until May 8.

We returned to Boston from a Western trip and opened a series with the Yankees on that date. Late in the game, Johnny Sain, the Yankee pitcher, who was a fine hitter, slammed one that was headed for the bull pen in right field. I got a good jump on the ball, ran with my back to the plate and, just before it dropped into the bull pen, managed to grab it. That catch saved the game, which we won in extra innings when Billy Goodman hit a home run.

Mickey Mantle, the Yankees' great switch hitter (a batter who hits from either the right or the left side of the plate), was batting right-handed the next day when he hit a ball to deep right-center field for what appeared to be an almost certain triple. The ball was headed for a corner formed by one side of the bull pen and the fence in front of the center-field bleachers. I ran back, and balancing myself with one hand against the bull pen, I reached over with the other and caught the ball. A veteran New York reporter wrote in his paper the next day, "In twenty-seven years of covering baseball, I never saw a catch like it."

Those two catches, along with plays I later made both at Fenway Park and in Yankee Stadium, seemed to convince Manager Casey Stengel of the Yankees that I was a great outfielder, and he later proved he felt that way when he picked me to play in the 1954 major-league all-star game in Cleveland. That was one of the big thrills of my life, for Stengel is a veteran baseball man who knows his business. The fans and the writers accepted me as a star, but I wanted recognition from someone who knew baseball from all its technical angles. When Casey selected me to play for him, I felt that I had really made the grade.

Early in the 1953 season, after he had seen me make those catches off Sain and Mantle, Stengel said, "Guess this Piersall must be the best outfielder in ten years, except for Willie Mays." When the season was over, he said, "Piersall is the best right fielder I've ever seen anywhere."

I robbed Mickey Vernon, who won the American League batting championship that year, of a sure triple in Washington. Later I took two home runs away from him on successive days in Boston. After I made the first of the two Fenway Park catches, Cronin is reported to have said, "That's the best catch I've ever seen." The next day, after I'd robbed Vernon again, they tell me Cronin said, "I take it back. *That* was the best catch I've ever seen." Incidentally, by that time, Vernon would gladly have strangled me.

In September, I hit the jackpot at Yankee Stadium. One day I took an extra-base hit from Irv Noren of the Yankees with a diving catch. The next day, I hoisted myself up on the edge of the bull pen with one hand and speared a long wallop by Joe Collins with the other, depriving him of a homer. On the day after, Hank Bauer hit one in the same general spot. Susce and Kinder, who were in the bull pen, were so sure that it was going in for a home run that they yelled, "No, no, Jimmy!" as I went after it. But when I made a stab for it anyhow, the ball landed in my glove, and it was just another out for Bauer. I guess it was that series that convinced Stengel.

When I took successive hits away from Al Rosen and Bob Lemon of the Indians in Cleveland the day I shut that heckler up, Bill McKechnie, our coach, said, "That kid gets balls Speaker wouldn't have reached." That was truly praise from Caesar, for McKechnie was a member of the old school of baseball men and Tris Speaker had been hailed for forty years as the greatest outfielder who ever lived.

Before the season was over, Boudreau told the writers one day, "I don't care if Piersall doesn't hit .240. He can play right field for me on his fielding alone."

Actually, I had a good year at the plate, ending up with a respectable, if not sensational, .272 batting average. I was satisfied. Between my opportunities to make miraculous catches and the very fact that I came back at all, I was the talk of baseball that year.

When the season was over, I was selected the outstanding Red Sox player of the year in a poll conducted by Leo Egan, sports announcer for Boston's radio station WBZ. He had set up a new award in Ted Williams's name, consisting of a silver bowl and a new Nash automobile. At the time, Williams had just returned from a second tour of duty in the United States Marine Air Corps. With Williams standing by, Egan made the presentation to me just before the season ended, and that was one of the thrills of my life. Later, to add frosting to the cake, the Associated Press, after conducting a poll among the nation's sports writers, named me as the outstanding sophomore player in the American League.

In his column, "Sports of the Times," Arthur Daly of the *New York Times* wrote:

"Piersall steals things. He steals singles, doubles, triples and homers from other ballplayers in the most blatant manner imaginable. Even when you see him do it, you think your eyes have been performing tricks on you. The youngster is incredible. He scales fences, swings on bullpen gates and teeters on low walls. But he always makes his catch.

"Piersall is a phenomenon in modern baseball, where the home-run hitter hitherto has ruled in solitary splendor as the gate attraction. The kid from Waterbury, Connecticut, packs 'em in just so they can watch him catch and throw a ball."

It was heartwarming to read words like that. Even

more heartwarming was a line in Harold Kaese's sports column in the *Boston Globe*, for it hit right home. Kaese wrote one day:

"More than any other player, the comeback big leaguer of 1953 is Jim Piersall, twenty-three-year-old Red Sox right fielder. He came from farther back than any of them."

I guess I *had* come from farther back than any of them and, perhaps, in a shorter time. But I still couldn't be really certain I had this thing licked until I had proved two things to myself. One was my ability to weather any real storm of adversity. The other was my ability to face the past in a manner that might help others.

The 1953 season was a remarkable one for me, but there was no particular reason why it shouldn't have been. Everything went my way. I was surrounded by people who wanted to help me. Mary, Dr. Brown, my close friends, Yawkey, Cronin, Susce, my own teammates, opposing players, umpires, writers, fans — everyone I could think of — had their hands out ready to pull me over the bumps and the hurdles. But the hurdles were very small. The highest was the little heckling I got in Cleveland, once the others had me all straightened out. I didn't get hurt, I didn't get into any fights, I didn't have to argue with the umpires and I didn't have to worry about what would appear in the newspapers.

I made some remarkable catches, but I couldn't have made them unless the ball was hit in my general direction. I made some good catches in 1954, but I didn't have half the chances that I had the previous year. But 1953 was

[205]

the big year for me. That was the season everyone was watching me to see if I *could* come back. That was the big year for me, and once it was over, I didn't have to worry about chances for great plays.

There was another factor in 1953 that didn't exist a year later. Our big guy was Ted Williams, and, shortly after we came North in 1952, Williams left to go back into the service. He didn't return until late in the 1953 season. Without Williams, the Red Sox had no big drawing card, no one to talk or write about. In his absence, fans and writers turned to me, and after a while every unusual catch or throw I made was big news. Then, when Williams returned, he naturally took over the spotlight, but not until he had loaned it to me at the precise time I needed it most — when encouragement and help from press and fans meant more than it ever could either earlier or later.

So I didn't have to meet the test of adversity at all in 1953 — there wasn't any adversity. Not until spring training in 1954 did I have to face an unpleasant reality. Then one day I ran into the fence and chipped a bone in my right wrist. It wasn't serious and I stayed out for only ten days, returning in time to open the season, but it would have worried me to death two years before. I took it in stride. Instead of thinking about the remote possibility that it might cause later complications, I calmly accepted the probability that the wrist would be as good as ever after the chip had healed.

But something happened in August that worried everybody who was interested in my future. We played an exhibition game with the New York Giants at Fenway Park, and one of the pregame features was a throwing contest between Willie Mays and me. Mays, the Giants' center fielder, was the most exciting young ballplayer of the 1954 season, a kid who could hit and throw and make out-of-this-world catches. Baseball followers often compared us as fielders, but never had a chance to see us in action at the same time, since the Giants are in the National League and the Red Sox in the American. So, for purposes of settling arguments for the moment, at least, this throwing contest was given a great deal of advance publicity.

There was a sellout crowd at Fenway Park, and I was anxious to make a good impression. We both stood in right center field, taking alternate fly balls, hit to us by Willard Nixon, one of our pitchers. We could throw to the plate from any angle, as long as we didn't go any closer than a point marked off by red stakes.

After I had made three or four throws, I ran in close to the stakes to take a shallow fly ball. It dropped in and out of my glove. In a hurry to get the ball away, I stopped, picked it up and threw it, all in the same motion. The minute the ball left my hand, I felt a twinge in the upper part of my back, just below my right shoulder. That was the end of the contest for me. I ran into the dugout.

I thought I had nothing more wrong with me than a tired shoulder, so I decided to play in the game, although the weather was threatening and a light rain was falling at the start. I went to right field wearing a rubber jacket over my uniform. In one of the early innings, I made a routine throw, and that time I felt a sharp pain. I got out of the game, went into the locker room for a heat treatment and hoped for the best. The next morning I woke up with a ballplayer's walking nightmare — a sore arm.

For nearly a month, I was plagued with the miseries in my arm. It was much more serious for me than it might be for other outfielders, since fielding rather than hitting was my long suit. A ball club can stand a light-hitting catcher or infielder, but normally, outfielders are expected to provide punch. As Arthur Daley had pointed out, I was a rare bird — an outfielder who attracted fans on his fielding alone. If I were a .300 hitter or a home-run slugger, I could get by with a poor arm. Not being either, a bad arm could knock me right out of the big leagues.

Now I really had something to worry about — but I didn't worry. At first, I hardly realized how casually I was taking what could be a major tragedy. I read a few stories labeled, "Is Piersall through?" and they didn't bother me in the least. I was certain that my arm would come around sooner or later. I worked out, rested it, played a little, and did everything the club doctor told me to. Just before the season ended, I knew my arm was all right again. I was throwing as well as ever and I suffered no twinges.

"If you can take that without worrying yourself to death, you can take anything," Mary remarked.

She was right. Once I had recovered from the arm ailment, I was confident that nothing would ever really bother me again.

EARLY in the 1953 season, I was faced with the prospect of being in a prime position to help others, but I wasn't sure whether I could handle it or not. When we arrived in Chicago on our first trip West, a man named Don Slovin phoned me at the Del Prado Hotel and asked to see me on a personal matter. We made arrangements to meet the next day. He turned out to be a fellow about my own age.

"I have recovered from a breakdown similar to the one you had," Slovin explained. "I now belong to a small group, all of whose members are in the same boat. They have either recovered from or have been threatened with a nervous or mental collapse. We call ourselves 'Fight Against Fears' and we meet periodically.

"We help each other just by letting down our hair and talking frankly about our troubles," he went on. "We don't have formal speeches or anything. We just get together, and when anyone has anything to say he says it. Sometimes somebody is very close to the line and desperately needs help, so we try to give it to him on the spot.

"There are about forty or fifty in our group. People who have had breakdowns aren't in a hurry to advertise it, so we know we only represent a small percentage of the recovered mental patients who live in the Chicago area. But we have succeeded pretty well in helping each other, and we think we can help a lot more people if they knew about the work we're doing.

"Now, Jimmy, you're the most famous former mental patient in the country, I guess — at least, I've never heard of anyone more famous who is willing to admit that he's been a mental patient. If you would come and talk to our group, you could not only help some of its members keep themselves from going off again, but you could help us find others who need us. What do you say?"

"What makes you think I'm willing to admit in public that I'm a graduate of a mental institution?" I asked.

"Well, everyone knows that you are. Are you sensitive about it? Have I said the wrong thing? If I have, please accept my apologies."

He got up to go, but I stopped him.

"No," I said, a little doubtfully. "You haven't said the wrong thing at all. You're a former mental patient yourself, so you must know how I feel."

"I think I do."

"Well, I haven't mentioned a word about my mental illness, except to members of my family and a few others who have helped me. I've been playing big-league ball and getting plenty of publicity on the sports pages, but everyone has studiously avoided the subject of my sickness. It never occurred to me that I could help anyone by talking about it, although I have felt that there are times when I'd like to discuss it with someone."

"We're a ready-made organization for you then," Slovin said. "You can help our people and yourself as well then by talking frankly. But I'll tell you this, Jimmy — you

[210]

can give a great deal more help than you'll get. You have had very special problems to face, and by telling our members how you've faced them, you'll be contributing heavily towards their peace of mind. I don't know how much they can contribute to yours."

"Let me think about it, Don," I said. "This is only our first trip into Chicago. We'll be in again soon. I'll give you an answer then."

I did a lot of thinking on the way around the circuit and then talked things over with Mary when I got home.

"Why shouldn't you do it?" she urged. "You're perfectly all right and maybe you really can be a help to people who are still shaky about their nerves. You've been through the wringer and it hasn't hurt you any. If you can help others, I think you should."

I wrote Slovin that I'd like to help his "Fight Against Fears" group, and he arranged a meeting to coincide with the Red Sox's next trip to Chicago. The moment I arrived at the meeting, I felt a warm glow in my heart. These men and women were my kind of people, for they had been where I had been, and knew exactly what I had gone through. They looked up to me, too, I found, because I could whip my problems while performing my daily work in a fishbowl of publicity and before thousands of people every day. It helped them to feel that they could perform theirs in the comparative privacy of their homes or their places of business.

I stood up and told them how everyone around me seemed anxious to help me come back, and that my fight was half won as soon as I learned to accept that fact. I told them that only a few were whispering behind my back and pointing a figurative finger of scorn at me, and that those few were lost in the shuffle.

"If you don't worry about the guy you think might hurt you, you'll find that he *can't* hurt you," I said. "I was a little afraid at first, but I found there was nothing to be afraid of. As soon as I realized that those fears were all in my head, I knew they really didn't exist at all. Now I don't have them any more."

After my talk, I sat around for a couple of hours while people fired questions at me, and I found that I could bring my own thoughts into sharp focus by trying to answer them. For example, a lady asked, "What do you do when things go badly for you?"

"I try to keep my temper," I replied.

"What if you feel yourself losing it?"

"I can stop myself before it goes too far."

"But what if you *can't* stop yourself?"

"If it gets that bad," I said, "I pray that I'll stop myself. That always works."

"Then you never lost your faith in God?"

"Never. God helped me face this situation and He led me out of it. I know He'll keep me out of it. Just telling Him my troubles is enough to relax me."

"Don't you ever get butterflies in your stomach?" a man asked.

"Sure I do. Everyone does at one time or another. You can get butterflies in your stomach doing anything."

"But what if they get so bad that you can't make them go away?"

"They'll go away if you face your problem squarely."

"But what if you can't make yourself face it?"

"There's no situation you can't face if you make up your mind to face it," I said.

On the way back to the hotel, Don said, "Jimmy, you were great. You were a real inspiration. Now how would you like to be an inspiration to people who don't know about 'Fight Against Fears'?"

"How?"

"By telling your story in public to Herb Kupcinet."

Kupcinet is a Chicago newspaper columnist who also conducts a local television program. I had heard of him and had watched his show, and I knew he was tremendously popular.

"Do you really think it will help?" I asked Don.

"I *know* it will."

"O.K. You arrange it."

The interview was short, but frank. I told Kupcinet's audience that I had been a victim of mental illness and had spent nearly two months in an institution, and that I was now completely cured. I pointed out the need for coming into the open and letting the world know that there were thousands like me, who could be cured if people would try to understand them. I also said that I was a member of "Fight Against Fears," and that we could help others if they wanted to join us. I added that I'd be personally glad to help anyone I could, and invited people with mental or emotional disturbances to write and tell me about them.

The result was instantaneous. The studio telephone

lines were jammed before we went off the air. Scores of people wanted to know about "Fight Against Fears" and where they could go to join it. Kupcinet was still getting inquiries about it a year later.

My own mail became so heavy that I had to get a secretary to help me answer it. Much of Kupcinet's mail was addressed to me in his care, and when I returned to Boston, I had over a hundred letters from Chicago people, nearly all of whom had been victims of some sort of mental illness. But one letter — not from a mental patient — made me particularly proud. It read, in part:

"Undoubtedly, you proved to be a source of inspiration to anyone who has gone through an experience similar to yours. But I might also suggest that you were also an inspiration to those who have other troubles and are finding difficulty in solving them. Like the philosopher who said something akin to, 'I must face the facts even though they may slay me,' you have faced the facts and slain them. And in the stark reality of day, you have gained the greatest of all victories — man's victory over himself.

"You resolved a possible tragedy into this ultimate victory. And though I shamefacedly admit little knowledge of your baseball ability, you have my deepest respect as one of the most courageous individuals about whom I have ever heard."

When I returned to Chicago for the first Western trip of 1954, "Fight Against Fears" had grown to five hundred in membership, all from the Greater Chicago area. They still meet regularly, still helping each other, and I enjoy meeting with them when I can. I spend all my spare time

[214]

with these people whenever I'm in Chicago, and just being with them is a heartwarming experience for me.

You can therefore imagine my pleasure when, on our first trip into Chicago last year, Kupcinet presented a plaque to me on his television show, in the name of the "Fight Against Fears" organization. It was the first of what will be an annual award to someone who contributes help to the group. The inscription reads:

"Presented to Jimmy Piersall for outstanding recovery and being inspirational example to others that they also may rise above their illness to become happier and more accomplished in their lives."

BASEBALL is, as I hope it will be for a long time, my principal means of livelihood, but it's no longer my only one. Thanks to the owners of the Colonial Provision Company in Boston, I have a good off-season job, which carries with it prospects of permanent employment when my baseball days are over. As a goodwill ambassador for the company, I cover most of New England, giving talks to many different kinds of groups. I was offered the job at the end of the 1953 season and it came at a time when I most needed that sort of lift. With a growing family — Mary and I now have four children and we had three then — I found myself faced with heavy responsibilities. Thanks to the Colonial people, I was never given time to worry about them.

The *Boston Globe* sent me to write a daily feature on

the 1953 World Series, between the Yankees and the Brooklyn Dodgers. It was a marvelous experience, because it gave me a chance to rub elbows with the newspapermen who had treated me with such consideration and tact. Incidentally, I also had a fine time for myself, thanks to the enthusiastic co-operation of the ballplayers on both teams. One New York writer, nowhere nearly as mad as he sounded in print, put it this way:

"As if we don't have troubles enough fighting off other writers, now we have to compete with a ballplayer for news. The Yankees and the Dodgers stand in line to be interviewed by Jimmy Piersall, while the rest of us get the leavings."

I was particularly happy when the *Globe* sent me to the 1954 World Series. The first time, it could have been a stunt. The second time, they obviously felt I could be of some use, and that meant a lot to me. That series was between the New York Giants and the Cleveland Indians, and I almost felt like a newspaperman while I was working on it.

But I knew I was Jimmy Piersall, the ballplayer who had returned from oblivion, when the airplane in which I was traveling took off from LaGuardia Airport for Cleveland halfway through the series. The stewardess came over and greeted me with a cheerful, "Hi, Jimmy, how are you?"

"Fine," I said, a little vaguely.

"Family all right?"

"Swell."

"Wife, children, everybody?"

"Yes."

"And how about you — are you happy now?"

"I'm very happy," I said.

"And I see you're playing the position you want to play. I'm glad of that."

"Uh-huh," I nodded.

Then she said, "Say, Jimmy, you don't seem to recognize me at all."

"I'm sorry. I don't remember ever having met you."

"Well, I was the hostess on the chartered plane the Red Sox took through Texas when they barnstormed on their way north from spring training in 1952."

"Gee," I said, "I don't remember much of anything that happened to me then. 1952 was a bad year for me."

"You mean because you were sick?"

"Yes."

"But wasn't that also the year that you were cured?" she asked.

"Yes, it was."

"Well, then, I'd say 1952 was a good year — the best of your life."

I guess maybe she was right, at that.

Afterword

Jim Piersall

I'm glad this book is back. It seems like the movie about it has run twice a year for the last thirty years. I don't like the movie, because the star doesn't look any bit of a ball player, but for forty years it has kept the story out there. The trouble is, most of the young people who know about me get their information from the movie, and the older people saw me play in Boston, Cleveland, L.A., New York, and Washington. And I played ball a lot better than the guys in the movie.

A lot has happened since the time in the book and the movie. I played some more in Boston, then Cleveland, then with Washington, and in 1963 I was with the Mets. Those early Mets had some trouble, but it was a good time. We had Duke Snider and some other older players that the fans liked to see back in New York. Duke was coming up on his 400th career home run, about the same time I was coming up on my 100th. I told Duke I would get more attention when I hit number 100 than he would get for 400. Now, they just laughed because Duke was big in New York from being on the Dodgers, and 400 is a lot of homers. So when I hit mine, I ran around the bases backwards, and it was all over the papers.

When the Mets let me go in 1963, we were in New York, and over in the American League, the Angels were in town to play the Yankees. So I went to see Bill Rigney, who was managing the Angels then. I told him that I was in shape and I could still play and that I thought I could help his club. He saw it the same way so he signed me.

Believe it or not, after the Angels left New York they went to Boston for a series. I was glad to be back in the American League, and the fans gave me a big hand the first time I came up to bat. Well Bill Rigney must have wondered what he had gotten into, because I got thrown out on one pitch. I'm up at the plate and I want to do good, to show both the Angels and the Boston fans they didn't make a mistake. Dick Radatz is pitching, and he's six feet seven. The first pitch was high, but the umpire called it a strike. Now, that seemed unfair. So I said to the ump, "He's a big guy, he doesn't need any help." I had the bat in my hand while I was arguing with him, the third base umpire came and grabbed the bat from my hand, he fell down, and I got thrown out.

I enjoyed playing with the Angels and got the comeback player of the year award the next year. So it did look like Rigney made a good move. I enjoyed playing for Rigney—he's a very happy guy, and I picked up a lot of knowledge about baseball from him. We were quite a team; we had Fregosi and Knoop and some kids who could play, and we had a bunch of older players—Frankie Malzone and Joe Adcock. We had fun—we trained in Palm Springs, what else could you want to do but spend the New Year in Palm Springs? I was there about seven years. It was an outstanding opportunity, and I really enjoyed myself. When I got through playing, I coached with Bill for awhile. Bill had played for the old New York Giants and managed a long time, and I'm glad he enjoyed me!

After I stopped playing, I thought that if I could diversify myself I could make a living in many different ways. I'm glad I can do different jobs, and I've had many times when I've had to go and sell myself to an employer and convince them I could do the job. I worked in the front office for the California Angels for a couple of years. Then I ran a football team for about three or four years. I had learned how to sell when

I was in Boston and had a food brokerage there. Then I worked for Charley Finley in Oakland for a year. It was one of the worst times of my life; check out the other book I wrote, *The Truth Hurts*. It still does. But it was a great experience, because the man was very clever, and I learned an awful lot about people. When I left there I managed for one summer, and then I got with my old friend Billy Martin in Arlington, Texas, where I worked in the front office selling and coached the Ranger outfielders.

After I left Texas, I auditioned to do the color commentary with Harry Caray for about two or three games, and I was able to win that job. Working with Harry for six years was a great experience. I learned a lot about sports broadcasting, and later, I had my own radio talk show six nights a week for a couple of years on WIND in Chicago. I'm proud that it was one of the highest rated drive-time shows in the city. During that time I was doing on-air TV broadcasting and promotions for the White Sox, while LaRussa was managing the team. You can read about my time with Tony in *The Truth Hurts*, too.

After that, all of a sudden I hooked an interview with Dallas Green over at the Cubs. And that's always made me grin, because he was pitching when I hit my 100th with the Mets. Dallas was looking for help with his coaching, he brought me in, and I made a presentation to him. I thought that I'd had enough of broadcasting work, so I told him that day, "I'll do the job for nothing if I have to, to prove I can do it." And that's what happened, and after about a month or so they hired me. That started my career with the Cubs, and we have been going for fourteen years now.

I've had the good fortune to work with kids like Rafael Palmeiro when he began as an outfielder (later they changed him into a first baseman), and Jerome Walton, and Doug Glanville as a rookie. Altogether I had fourteen young people who I helped with their development to become major league players. That's been quite a thrill. Right now I'm working with a talented kid—Cory Patterson, signed as an outfielder. He's capable of earning the money they've given him. He's got the attitude, he's got the ability to learn, and he's a very quick learner. He's in the instructional league in Arizona now. They send the young ones out for about five weeks in the fall. We play ball games with other clubs' kids, and they get instruction at the same time.

Now I roam all over the country for the Cubs. I spend the summers with the six teams the Cubs have, and I go through them all periodically. I talk baseball with these kids. I talk reality with them. I talk to them about what it takes—and not just in the game. One kid was going around saying, "I'm not going to be a power hitter," and "I can't field good," and I told him, "No, you hit .300 in A ball, and you're nineteen years old, and you're going to make millions of dollars. Just keep playing as best you can." He had a great year, and he is still nineteen—a kid.

Kids will talk to me because they know I won't talk behind their backs, and lots of times I've told them to go and get a job. I say, "If after three years you don't have the credentials, you don't have a future. If you're not out of the A level after three years, it's time to start your career in something else, because you've got to live." To me, you've got to put some numbers on the board, to have shown by then what you can do. Pitchers take a little longer, but I don't really get involved with too many pitchers. The only thing I know about pitchers is that I could hit 'em!

I was a good fielder too. My lifetime fielding average was .997. It doesn't seem right that the record books got me at .990, because I made ten errors at shortstop when they had me play there that first year. I don't know how many games I played there, but they put them in along with my fielding in the outfield. I called the Encyclopedia people a few years ago.

and they said they would change it, but they never did. They just put it all together no matter what position you played, which doesn't really tell you anything.

Once I established myself, I could see that the fans would stand and give ovations. You don't see fielders get ovations like they give these home run hitters, but I was getting them coming out of the field after I made some catches. Time and time again I had an opportunity to make big plays. A lot of times you could play all year and not really show your ability because you got a lot of easy chances.

So I tell these kids, "Don't ever give up on a ball. Don't go three-quarters out. Don't ever say, 'What the hell,' when the ball looks likes it's hit out, just keep running. You don't know what is going to happen." That's why my kids make a lot of outstanding plays.

My first year in the majors Casey Stengel picked me for the All-Star team, so the whole thing was wonderful for me. My biggest opportunity came when I played my first exhibition game that spring against the Dodgers—Carl Erskine was pitching and I was five for five. The first baseman was Gil Hodges, second base was Jackie Robinson, the shortstop was Pee Wee Reese, Bobby Cox was at third, Campanella catching, Gene Hermanski in left, Snider in center, and Furillo in right. That's a pretty good ball club. That was a real turning point. Because I had fears in my mind whether I could really play or not.

I was very fortunate that Mr. Yawkey sent me to Florida later, as you read in *Fear Strikes Out.* George Susce, a coach who lived down there, kept saying, "You're the best right fielder around." That really helped me because all during my career I had the fear of someone taking my job.

This is what I try to tell the kids. You can't be complacent and think, "well my mother or father will take care of me for a year when I get home." You've got to go out and play every game like it's the World Series, you've got to produce, and your competition means only seven percent of you make it. Don't loaf, don't put your head down when you strike out. All these things I've learned to communicate with these kids. They know I don't stand for someone coming to me at eight o'clock in the morning without enthusiasm and a desire to learn. I tell them to listen when I'm making corrections and don't be embarrassed if I pull you over to teach something. But they understand.

Kids are great. Kids today are smart as hell, and if you know what you're talking about, they'll listen. They respect you. And every morning that I come in, they say, "Good morning, Jim," and I kid with them, and it's really keeping me alive. Which is why I don't plan to retire. I wouldn't be very happy about it. I'm not prepared to sit around the house and watch television all day.

Baseball is better than ever too. Everybody can play baseball, whether they play with a tennis ball or rubber ball or with toilet paper or whatever. Half of the fans in the stands are women. In baseball there are so many home runs there is tremendous excitement now. I can't believe how much better the players get each year. And everyone is talking about baseball again—asking "who are you rooting for?" I love it.

I started out as a guy without an education. But because of baseball and an ability to work hard, I have done all right just the same. So when they say about me, "Is he really nuts?" I can say I worked hard all my life, I fought my fears, and I was determined to win. And I'm a happy man.

Jimmy Piersall